CW01334989

MEASURING CREDIT RISK

MEASURING CREDIT RISK

Brian Coyle

CIB PUBLISHING

BPP
FINANCIAL EDUCATION

Apart from any fair dealing for the purpose of research or private study, or criticism or review, as permitted under the Copyright, Designs and Patents Act 1988, this publication may only be reproduced, stored or transmitted, in any form or by any means, with the prior permission in writing of the publisher, or in the case of reprographic reproduction in accordance with the terms and licences issued by the Copyright Licensing Agency. Enquiries concerning reproduction outside those terms should be addressed to the publisher's agents at the undermentioned address:

CIB Publishing
c/o The Chartered Institute of Bankers
Emmanuel House
4-9 Burgate Lane
Canterbury
Kent
CT1 2XJ
United Kingdom

Telephone: 01227 762600

CIB Publishing publications are published by The Chartered Institute of Bankers, a non-profit making registered educational charity.

The Chartered Institute of Bankers believes that the sources of information upon which the book is based are reliable and has made every effort to ensure the complete accuracy of the text. However, neither CIB, the author nor any contributor can accept any legal responsibility whatsoever for consequences that may arise from errors or omissions or any opinion or advice given.

Typeset by The Foundry
Printed by WBC Book Manufacturers, Bridgend

© Chartered Institute of Bankers 2000

ISBN 0-85297-450-7

Contents

1.	Controlling Credit Risk	1
2.	Methods of Credit Assessment	15
3.	Credit Rating Agencies	23
4.	External Information Sources	41
5.	In house Credit Assessments	49
6.	Industry Risk and Country Risk	63
7.	The Assessment of Banks	73
8.	Setting and Policing Credit Limits	91
9.	Credit Deterioration	105
10.	Conclusion	115
Glossary		121
Index		127

Controlling Credit Risk

The nature of credit risk is explained in some detail in *Framework for Credit Risk Management*, another title in this series. Briefly, credit risk is the possibility that loss could arise from non-payment or late payment of a financial obligation by a customer.

Who is Exposed to Credit Risk?

The credit risk for banks consists of the amounts owed by borrowers on loans for both interest payments and loan principal repayments, and also for customers' debts on other transactions, such as swaps, letters of credit, performance bonds or forward rate agreements (FRAs). Other companies are similarly exposed to the risk of non-payment or late payment from customers for goods or services supplied on credit.

Companies also could be exposed to some credit risk in their dealings with a bank.

If a company is cash-rich and places money on deposit with a bank, there could be the risk of the bank going into liquidation, and the company losing most of its deposits. There is also an interest-rate risk in placing too much money on deposit with a single bank. The bank, aware that a company is a regular depositor, might not offer an interest rate on new deposits as high as the rate that could be obtained from a different bank.

Example
Alpha Inc has an overdraft facility of $4 million from Omega Bank and is overdrawn by $3.5 million on its account. Omega Bank decides to cut Alpha's facility to $2 million.

Analysis
Unless Alpha can reduce its overdraft from $3.5 million to $2 million immediately, and that is unlikely, its directors will be forced to put the company into liquidation. Otherwise they would be liable for allowing the company to trade while insolvent.

Credit Exposures

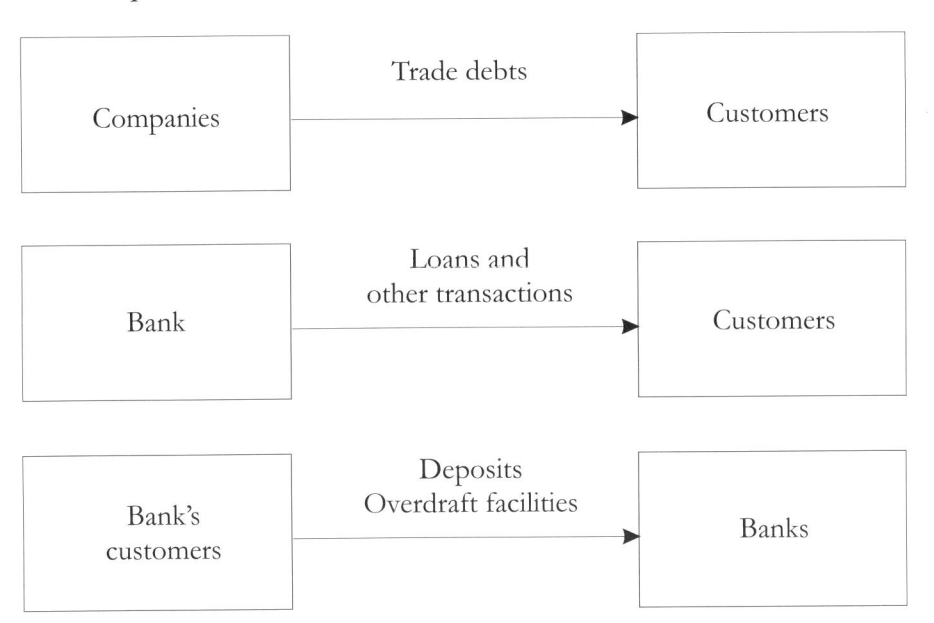

Companies	→ Trade debts →	Customers
Bank	→ Loans and other transactions →	Customers
Bank's customers	→ Deposits / Overdraft facilities →	Banks

Size and Duration of Credit Risk

Exposure to credit risk lasts for the duration of the credit period. With a trade debt, this is from the time of sale to the receipt of payment from the sale. If goods are made or projects are designed to a customer's specification, the credit risk begins earlier, as soon as the supplier starts to spend money on the contract. With a bank loan, the period of credit exposure is the remaining term to maturity of the loan.

The size of the credit risk is the amount that could be lost if the risk were to be realized, and non-payment or late payment occurred. The maximum potential loss is the full amount of the debt in the event of non-payment by the customer. With a trade debt, non-payment would result in a loss of the full amount owed. A bad debt on a bank loan would create a loss of the unpaid debt principal, plus any overdue, unpaid interest.

In an extreme case, a customer bad debt could force a company into liquidation. This could occur when the bad debt is for a large amount, and the company had been relying on payment to settle its own debts to suppliers or its bank.

When a bad debt occurs, the actual loss could be less than the full amount owed. Unpaid creditors might receive some payment on liquidation of the debtor's assets, although unsecured creditors in particular could have to wait a long time for any such payment.

Unlike bad debts, late payments do not result in a direct loss. However, there is an indirect loss; the interest cost of having to finance debtors for longer than necessary, or the loss of interest that could have been earned from the money if it had been received sooner and placed on deposit.

Example
Beta sells $6 million of goods and services to Gamma, at a regular monthly rate of $500,000. Gamma has arranged credit terms of 30 days from the invoice date, but invariably takes two months to pay. Beta has a loan, and pays interest at 12% per annum.

Analysis
Because Gamma takes longer credit than allowed (an extra month), Beta has $500,000 less in cash than should be the case. Beta is permanently financing extra debtors of $500,000. The cost to Beta in interest charges is $60,000 per annum (12% × $500,000).

Risk and Return

When a company has $1 million of trade debtors, or when a bank has $1 billion of loans to customers outstanding, the potential credit risk is, in theory at least, the full amount of the debts or loans. In practice, however, only a small proportion of debts will be unpaid. Most customers will pay in full, and the actual loss will be the small proportion of bad debts plus the interest cost from the much larger proportion of late payments.

The concern for credit managers is the risk of bad debts from marginal customers, and the potential cost of overdue payments.

A company might choose to offer more attractive credit terms to customers, in the expectation of increasing its sales turnover. The intended benefit of this policy would be the extra profit from the higher sales. The potential risk is that a large proportion of the additional customers could be a high debt risk. Similarly, a bank could increase the size of its loan book, but the new customers to which it lends could be a bigger credit risk than its existing customer base.

A downturn in the economy also will increase bad debts. Bank losses on company loans and mortgages in times of recession are a clear illustration of how an adverse change in economic conditions can result in higher-than-expected losses as a higher proportion of loans fall into arrears and many eventually are written off.

Although the credit risk is greater for marginal lending and marginal trade credit, banks and companies must grant credit to make profits. Companies must give trade credit to win sales. For a bank, lending money is a profit-making activity in itself.

Some credit risk therefore is unavoidable, because without risk there is no return. Banks can compensate themselves for the extra risk on marginal lending by demanding a higher return, that is by charging higher rates of interest.

Nevertheless, decisions have to be taken about how much credit should be granted, and whether giving more credit would be justifiable in view of the higher potential returns, or too risky in view of the high potential losses on the marginal business.

The aim of credit management should be to contain the level of credit risk. At any given volume of sales or lending, the risk can be contained. Systems can be established to identify unacceptable risk before credit is given, so that the request for credit can be refused. Once credit has been granted, the customer's situation can be monitored, and any signs of deterioration in the customer's position, e.g. late payments can be identified early. Rigorous debt collection procedures also can be installed.

The purpose of this book is to focus on methods of credit assessment, setting credit limits and credit monitoring.

Warning Signs of Credit Risk

A key function of credit management is to identify high-risk customers. Bankers probably would argue that the origins of bad debts happen during times when the economy is strong. Companies are profitable, have a confident outlook for the future, and seek loans to expand their businesses. Banks, judging companies on their current profitability and with equal optimism for the future, have been willing to lend. But when the economy takes a downturn, the optimism disappears, profits shrink and companies struggle to meet their loan commitments. By this time, it is too late. The loans have been granted, and the bad debts are difficult to avoid. A problem for banks is how to decide during the good times of profitability whether the company would be a high credit risk if its business were to decline, or fail to grow quickly enough.

In contrast, the credit risk in decisions to lend when the economy is at the bottom of a recession could be much lower. If a company is making profits in recession, it is likely to survive and prosper in the future, when economic conditions improve. Poor lending decisions in a recession therefore should be much less common than during the years of economic growth.

According to one banker's metaphor, the seeds of credit risk are sown in the times of prosperity, and the harvest of bad debts is reaped in the winter of business depression.

Credit managers and bankers will have their own views on why bad debts occur, and when a credit decision is at fault. Bad debts can occur because of adverse changes in a customer's circumstances that might or might not have been anticipated, but bad debts also can occur because of weaknesses in the credit-granting process.

The following examples often are given as the most frequent causes of bad lending decisions

- over trading by the borrower
- adverse trading for the borrower
- a liquidity run on the borrower's business
- excessive capital commitments by the borrower
- faulty credit analysis by the lender
- creative accounting by the borrower, masking the business's true financial position
- deceit by the borrower.

The first three reasons could arise from changing circumstances in the borrower's business after the initial lending decision has been made. Even so, the warning signs of risk should be evident from the beginning.

The fourth reason, excessive capital commitments, can occur fairly suddenly and without warning for the lending bank. The final three reasons are not the result of changing circumstances in the borrower's business, but mainly are because of faulty lending decisions by the bank.

Over Trading

As the term suggests, over trading occurs when a company is over-extending its resources, and trying to support too much business volume with too little capital funding. A typical symptom of over trading is an increasing reliance on trade credit and a bank loan to support a rapid increase in stock levels and unpaid debtors. A business that depends increasingly on short-term credit, taking longer to pay suppliers and tax bills, and extending its loans eventually will suffer a cash flow crisis. Unpaid creditors could demand immediate payment, or the bank could withdraw loan facilities.

Adverse Trading

Business costs can be analyzed into fixed costs and variable costs. Fixed costs are monthly or annual expenditures that remain much the same in total, despite any rise or fall in business activity during the period. Variable costs, in contrast, are expenditures that increase when sales volume rises, and decline when sales volume falls.

Companies whose costs are largely fixed can benefit from a large increase in profits when sales volume rises, but are vulnerable to any downturn in sales. If sales volume falls, income will be less, but costs will remain at much the same level. Profits and net cash flows therefore would be lower. Companies with a high fixed-cost base and operating in a market where sales volume is volatile, are potentially vulnerable and a high credit risk.

Example
Delta has annual fixed expenditures of $3.5 million. It also has variable expenditures equal to 10% of sales turnover. Sales turnover is currently $4 million per annum.

Analysis
Delta currently is trading at a profit, as shown below, but it has a high volume of fixed costs relative to variable costs.

	$	% of revenue
Fixed costs	3,500,000	87.5
Variable costs (10% of $4 million)	400,000	10.0
Total costs	3,900,000	97.5
Profit	100,000	2.5
Sales	4,000,000	100.0

For each $1 increase in sales, Delta's profit would increase by 90¢ because extra variable costs would be just 10¢. For each $1 fall in sales, however, profit also would fall by 90¢.

Therefore Delta is vulnerable to a decline in sales below the current level. If sales fell by 10%, for example, to $3.6 million per annum, the company would make a loss, as follows:

	$
Fixed costs	3,500,000
Variable costs (10% of $3.6 million)	360,000
Total costs	3,860,000
Sales	3,600,000
Loss	(260,000)

The risk in giving credit or lending to Delta would depend on the volatility of Delta's sales. If sales are likely to fluctuate sharply up or down, the risk of business failure could be very high.

Liquidity Run

Occasionally, for an unexpected and unforeseeable reason, a company could suffer a loss of an income source, or a step-up in spending. Food manufacturers, for example, can suffer from a rumor or a news story about food poisoning or a health risk that can sharply reduce their sales volumes as consumers stop buying the product concerned. Supermarkets could take a decision to stop stocking a manufacturer's item and switch to an alternative from a rival producer. Events such as these can strain a company's cash flows, even if the loss of income or higher spending is short-lived. Although a lending bank cannot predict a run on a company's liquidity, it can assess whether the company could have sufficient liquidity or access to extra funds to survive any setback to its cash flows.

Excessive Capital Commitments

Companies might take on excessive capital commitments, and sign contracts for large-scale expenditures. If the company is unable to honor its commitments, it could be forced into liquidation. Lending banks and suppliers of trade credit often are unable to control a company's excessive spending, but can try to monitor it by looking at the most recent published accounts of the company for example, where capital expenditure commitments must be disclosed.

Faulty Credit Analysis

A bank can make a bad lending decision, not because of an unexpected change in the borrower's circumstances, but because the borrower was a high risk from the outset. The original lending decision could be flawed. There is always some risk of bad decisions on the basis of information available, but the frequency of bad loans can be contained by means of a structured approach to lending by trained staff.

Creative Accounting

Creative accounting is a term used to describe the use of corporate accounting policies that put a misleading gloss on a company's reported financial position. Profits can be made to seem larger, assets can seem more valuable, and liabilities sometimes can be hidden and kept off balance sheet. Creative accounting techniques are discussed in *Corporate Credit Analysis*, another title in this series. They include capitalizing interest costs within fixed assets costs and capitalizing development costs as fixed assets instead of charging the costs against profit, and methods of charging costs direct to reserves (reserve accounting) instead of recording them through the year's profit and loss account.

It is important for credit managers to be aware that many companies will take advantage of opportunities for creative accounting, if they exist. A credit manager should know, in broad terms at least, what those opportunities are, and should be able to identify the signs that a company is using them.

When a bad debt occurs through the failure of a company that used creative accounting techniques, the credit provider should take some of the blame.

Character of the Borrower

Occasionally, a borrower can deceive a lender, with the deliberate intention of creating a bad debt. Lenders need to be wary of this possibility and try to make a judgment from objective information about the borrower's character.

A case history is given below to illustrate how a bank can be deceived by a borrower, even when it thinks that its security and loan covenants will provide protection against credit risk.

Example
Able is an individual who owns 100% of a company called Romeo. The company is making losses, and Able approaches Foxtrot Bank with a request for a $3 million loan to Romeo, to enable Romeo to purchase Sierra, a profitable trading company in the same industry.

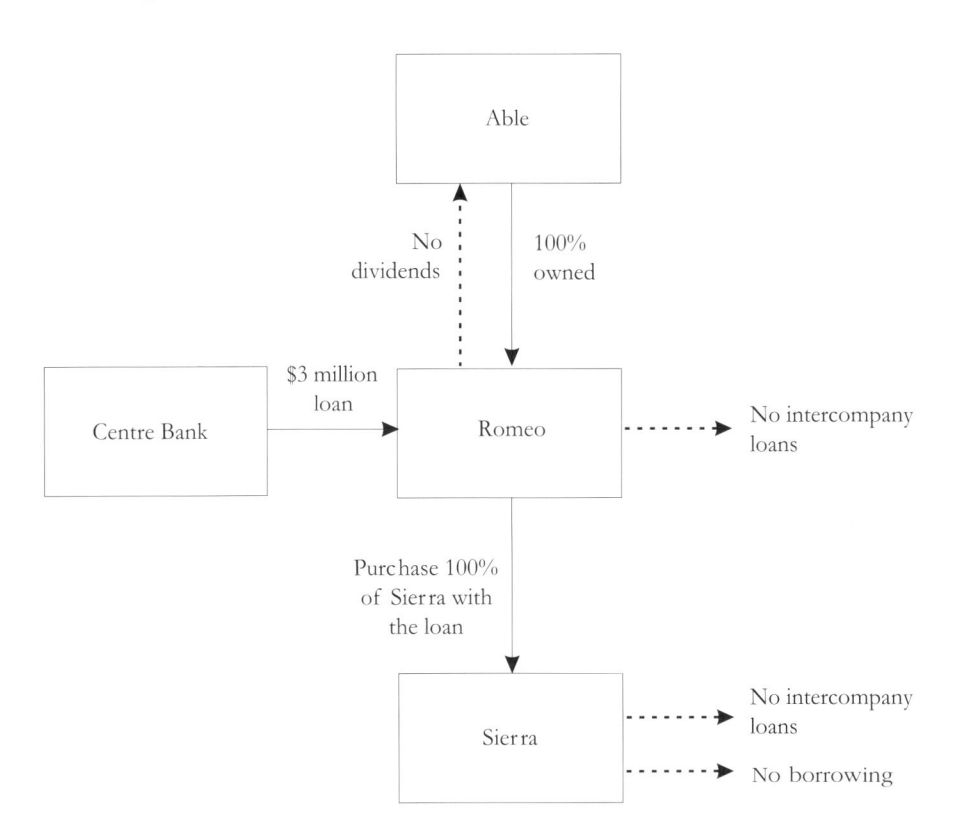

```
                            ┌─────────┐
                            │  Able   │
                            └─────────┘
                         ▲              │
                    No   │              │ 100%
                 dividends              owned
                         │              ▼
┌──────────┐ $3 million ┌─────────┐
│  Centre  │    loan    │         │ ----> No intercompany
│   Bank   │ ─────────▶ │  Romeo  │         loans
└──────────┘            └─────────┘
                             │
                    Purchase 100%
                    of Sierra with
                       the loan
                             ▼
                        ┌─────────┐
                        │         │ ----> No intercompany
                        │ Sierra  │         loans
                        │         │ ----> No borrowing
                        └─────────┘
```

MEASURING CREDIT RISK

Foxtrot Bank agrees, but insists on certain loan conditions. Romeo cannot pay any dividends to Able, nor make any inter-company loans to other companies in the group, until the loan is repaid. Similarly, Sierra cannot make any inter-company loans, nor take on any further external borrowings.

Able also owns 100% of Tango, another separate company, that has a loss-making subsidiary, Victor. Able makes an arrangement whereby Victor becomes a subsidiary of Sierra in exchange for 78% of Sierra's share capital being transferred to Tango. Foxtrot Bank is not informed of this transaction by Able.

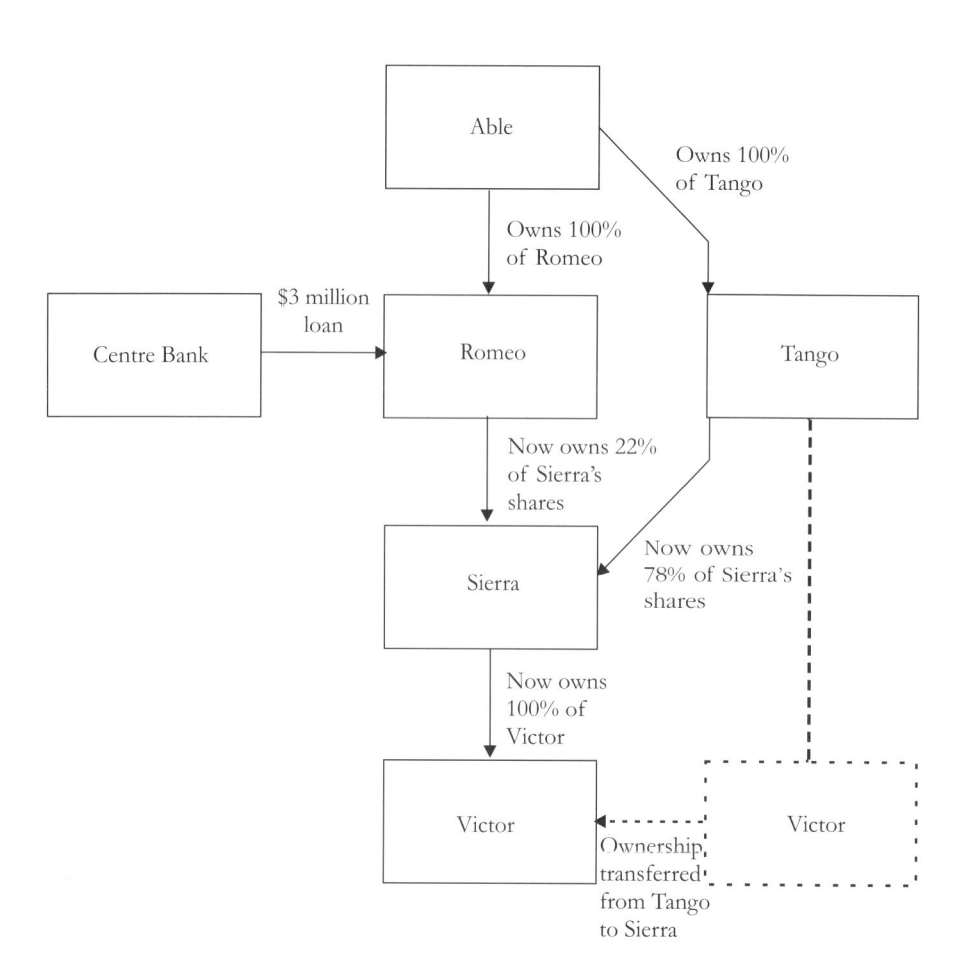

Able now arranges for Tango to borrow $2 million from another bank, Omega Bank, secured against Tango's 78% shareholding in the profitable company, Sierra. Foxtrot Bank is not informed of this by Able. Tango then pays the $2 million in cash to Able.

A few months later, the losses of Romeo and Victor force the entire Romeo group into liquidation, in spite of the profits of Sierra. Foxtrot Bank is an unpaid creditor of Romeo for $3 million.

Tango also goes into liquidation, owing $2 million to Omega Bank.

Analysis
Able, by acting deceitfully towards Foxtrot Bank and Omega Bank, has pocketed $2 million. Each bank can claim against Romeo and Tango respectively, but the banks must fight over the only assets with any potential value, the shareholding of each company in Sierra.

Omega Bank would have the prior claim on Sierra's assets over Foxtrot Bank, because of the mortgage on 78% of Sierra's shares. Foxtrot Bank, the original lending bank, could end up with a bad debt for the full $3 million loan.

Summary
Credit managers must understand the causes of business failure and bad debts and should be able to carry out a credit risk assessment on any customer. The assessment should look for information that could be evidence of a bad debt risk.

Credit assessments can be obtained from various sources or carried out in several different ways.

Methods of Credit Assessment

The purpose of credit assessment is to control the risk in credit decisions. For providers of credit, a credit assessment provides a basis for a decision about whether credit should be granted. Continuing assessments can then help the credit manager to monitor the customer's account. For large, cash-rich companies, an assessment of banks can help to decide how much cash to deposit with each bank. For companies seeking to borrow, an assessment of several banks can sometimes guide a decision about which bank to approach for a loan.

Sources of Assessment

Credit assessments can be obtained externally, from specialist agencies, or carried out inhouse by an organization's own staff.

Many large companies, banks and also governments and government agencies, have credit ratings for their existing debt. Ratings are provided by agencies such as Moody's, Standard & Poor's and IBCA. Banks can use a company's credit rating in deciding what rate of interest to charge on new borrowing by the company. For example, a company with a lower rating would be charged a higher rate of interest. Companies can use banks' credit ratings to decide its deposit limits with each bank.

Credit ratings apply only to large organizations. Credit information about smaller businesses can be obtained from a variety of sources, such as credit reference agencies. Agencies charge a small fee, but stay in business because they provide a useful and economical service. Other external assessments, such as a banker's reference, provided by the customer's bank, might be less detailed and so less reliable.

An inhouse credit analysis will use many of the same basic techniques as external agencies. Credit analysts will monitor a company or bank by

- collecting any available published information about the company and its management, including newspaper and magazine articles and television reports
- keeping an eye on the company's stock market performance in the case of listed public companies
- analyzing the company's business risk, its strengths and weaknesses in resources and management, and the threats and opportunities in its industry and markets
- analyzing the company's financial position, as disclosed in available financial statements. A financial assessment would be based perhaps on financial ratio analysis, and possibly also a points-scoring system for risk assessment.

Financial Assessment

An assessment of a company's financial position is often based on historical accounting information extracted from its annual report and accounts. Much of this information relates to profits and balance sheet values for assets and liabilities. The credit analyst is mainly concerned with the probability that the company will have sufficient to pay what it owes on time.

A problem with financial ratio analysis is that historical information about profits, assets and liabilities is used for an assessment of a future cash flow position. In the diagram overleaf the analyst starts from Point A to get to Point B.

Financial Ratio Analysis

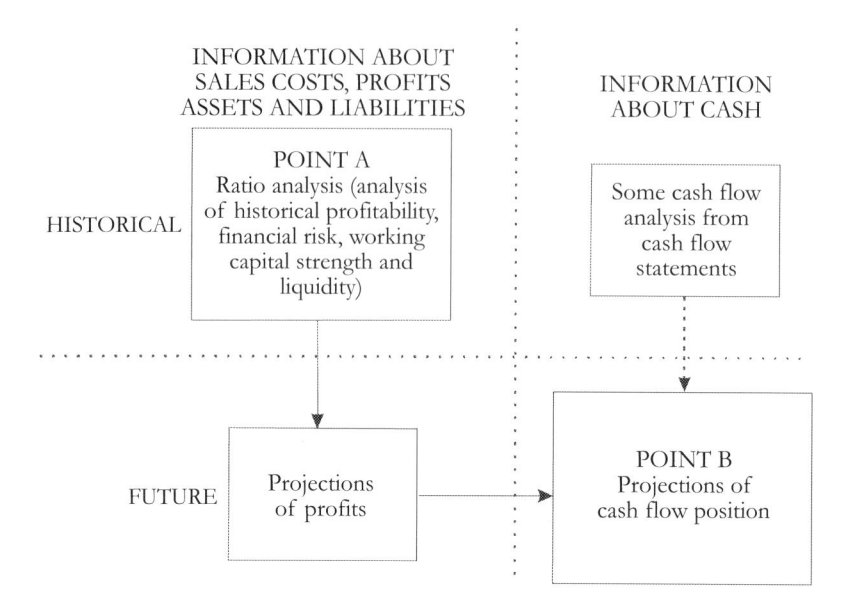

```
                 INFORMATION ABOUT
                 SALES COSTS, PROFITS          INFORMATION
                 ASSETS AND LIABILITIES        ABOUT CASH

                      POINT A
                 Ratio analysis (analysis      Some cash flow
                 of historical profitability,  analysis from
  HISTORICAL     financial risk, working       cash flow
                 capital strength and          statements
                 liquidity)


                                                    POINT B
                      Projections               Projections of
  FUTURE              of profits                cash flow position
```

In some cases, credit analysts could consider a portfolio of credit risks, to assess whether too much credit is being given to customers in particular industries or in particular countries. Some form of industry risk analysis or country risk analysis therefore could be required, although these forms of analysis are perhaps more directly relevant to investment analysts rather than credit analysts, because they are based mainly on a longer-term view of risk.

The assessment of banks by credit analysts in large companies should consider the capital adequacy of the banks. Rules on capital adequacy for banks have been set out under an international agreement known as the Basle Agreement. These capital adequacy requirements could restrict the ability of some banks to increase the size of their loan book, and could even force banks on occasion to reduce their volume of lending.

Choosing Between External and Internal Assessment Methods

A range of assessment methods is illustrated in the following diagram. The most suitable blend of inhouse and external sources of information will depend on circumstances, although the track record of past payments is always an important credit guide for existing customers.

Sources of Credit Information

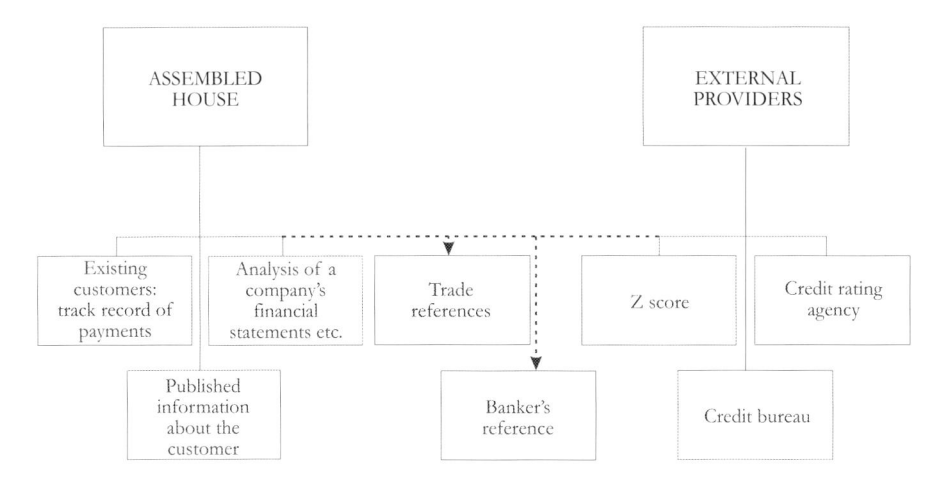

```
                ASSEMBLED                                    EXTERNAL
                  HOUSE                                      PROVIDERS

   Existing      Analysis of a
  customers:      company's        Trade                                    Credit rating
track record of   financial      references        Z score                     agency
  payments       statements etc.

                  Published
                 information                       Banker's
                  about the                       reference              Credit bureau
                  customer
```

For the business of a sole trader or a partnership, published accounts are unavailable. The services of a suitable credit information agency might be appropriate for these types of customer.

For each sizeable corporate customer seeking trade credit above a certain limit, it would be preferable to rely on an inhouse assessment of its published accounts instead of, or in addition to, using an external agency. An inhouse assessment helps the credit manager to understand the customer's business better, and to monitor its progress over time. However, if the work load would be too high to do the task inhouse, a credit information agency could be used. Agencies also can be used to gather and supply relevant information about a corporate customer, at relatively little cost.

For very big orders where the customer probably will have to obtain a loan to pay for the goods, the customer's status as a large-scale borrower is significant. It will affect the interest rate at which the customer could borrow, and will be a guide to the customer's credit risk. This type of credit assessment is commonplace for manufacturers of big ticket items and also for major building and engineering contracts, defense equipment manufacturers, and so on. A credit rating agency, such as Moody's or S&P, can be an invaluable guide for credit decisions for foreign customers, including foreign governments. Similarly, for very large borrowings, the choice of bank or banks from which to ask for a loan could be assisted by a credit rating assessment from an agency such as Fitch IBCA.

Z-scoring is a statistical method for assessing a company's financial strength, as well as the possibility that it might fail. The score is derived from a number of key financial ratios, each given a particular weighting in the Z score model. Companies with a Z score below a certain level would be considered a potentially high credit risk. Z scores are possibly useful for long-term credit decisions, and could help banks in particular. Banks, however, will have their own opinions about the reliability of Z score assessments, and will use them, or a similar credit-scoring model, to a greater or lesser extent accordingly, probably as just one element in their credit analysis of customers.

Using Financial Assessments

Financial assessments are used to reach credit decisions. Risk can be quantified, and where appropriate, limits set for lending, giving trade credit, or depositing cash. Limits can be applied to the total credit amount, to individual companies or banks, and to groups of companies, e.g. an industry limit, or banks, e.g. a country limit.

The credit provider can limit the risk by insisting on some form of security or guarantee. Bank loans could be secured on the borrower's fixed and floating assets. Loan guarantees could be obtained from a third party.

Companies could take out credit-risk insurance. Alternatively, they could insist on a method of payment where the risk should be minimal, e.g. confirmed letters of credit. Risk could be avoided completely by insisting on payment in advance, but only if enough customers agree to these terms of business.

Credit limits, once set, should be monitored to ensure that they are not breached. Credit managers should also monitor carefully individual credit transactions for overdue payments, and watch for signs of credit deterioration.

Companies and banks can choose from a variety of methods of credit assessment. The choice of method, if any is used, will depend on circumstances, such as the amount of credit involved, the length of the credit period and the availability of information. In the chapters that follow, a number of the assessment methods are described in some detail. Business risk assessments and financial assessments, financial ratio analysis etc., are dealt with in *Corporate Credit Analysis*, another title in this series.

Credit Rating Agencies

A rating is a formal opinion, given by a credit rating agency, of the creditworthiness of an entity that could be a government, government agency, financial institution or large company. Ratings provide a basis for comparing the credit risk of one organization with the risk of others.

The Purpose of Credit Ratings

The main purpose of credit ratings is to provide information to investors in public issues of debt capital, such as eurobonds. A rating is a guide to the investment risk. This is the probability that investors will receive interest payments in full and on time and repayment of the principal when the debt reaches maturity.

Investors can base their investment policy on credit ratings, restricting the amount that fund managers can invest in debt capital below a certain credit rating, or even prohibiting investment in issues with a rating below a certain level.

In addition, the rating of any company's existing debt issues will greatly affect the interest rate at which the organization can go into the markets to raise extra funds.

Credit ratings have gained a more widespread acceptance, outside investment analysis. Banks can look at the credit rating for the debt securities of a company and decide whether to lend to that company, and if so at what rate of interest. The margin above LIBOR at which large companies can negotiate loans is influenced by the credit rating system.

Banks also can use credit ratings to set limits on the value of transactions with a company. For example, a bank might set a limit on the size of a loan, the amount of a performance bond, or the size of FX transaction, and so on, for any company with a given credit rating.

Credit ratings also can have public relations implications, because ratings of different organizations can be compared. As a result companies and banks with top credit ratings can present themselves as élite organizations within their industry.

How do Ratings Come About?

Ratings are provided by specialist agencies. The major international credit rating agencies are Standard & Poor's and Moody's, and the UK-based Fitch IBCA.

Credit rating agencies, on request, will carry out a rating exercise, normally on an international organization that makes an issue of debt capital. The request for a rating comes from an issuer of new debt capital, e.g. an issue of bonds, or its financial advisers.

The rating exercise is carried out on the issuer, but the rating is applied to the specific debt issue, once the documentation for the issue has been reviewed. In other words, the credit rating is applied not to an organization itself, but to its debt securities. However, it is usual for investors and financiers to refer to the creditworthiness of organizations themselves in terms of the credit rating of their debt. A highly rated company could be referred to as a triple-A rated company.

The rating for an issue is kept under review, and if the creditworthiness of the issuer declines or improves, the rating will be changed accordingly.

Example
Aerospatiale, through its state ownership and importance to France as an aerospace and defense contractor, has a higher rating from Standard and Poor's than would be possible from a strict consideration of its financial

position only. Similar reasoning is behind the AAA ratings on long-term debt issued by SNCF and EDF even though their future borrowings no longer carry the guarantee of the French government.

The Rating Process for a Company

Once a credit rating agency receives a request from a company for a formal credit rating, it begins a preliminary assessment. This involves a review of about five years of published financial results and other publicly available information about the company, such as press releases. Financial ratios are calculated and analyzed, and comparisons are made with the company's industrial peer group. Trends in financial ratios over the period are also studied. Standard & Poor's gives this analysis of historical results a weighting of about 40% in the final credit rating decision.

The preliminary assessment is discussed with the company before a detailed review begins. The company is told about the likelihood of it obtaining the sought-after credit rating. An agreement to carry out a more detailed review will be given only if the company is willing to carry on at this stage.

Much time is spent in discussions between the company's senior management and the agency's investigators. Through such discussions, the agency should obtain a much better picture of the company's position, and its creditworthiness than from a study of public data alone. However, an agency probably will admit that the standard of these investigations depends on the amount and quality of the information given by the company's management. A Standard & Poor's manager has commented, "if an annual report and accounts provides the bones of an analysis, we also have full access to the flesh! We are thus able to achieve a far greater understanding of a company's creditworthiness than is possible through the analysis of external material alone".

Stages in the Credit Rating Process

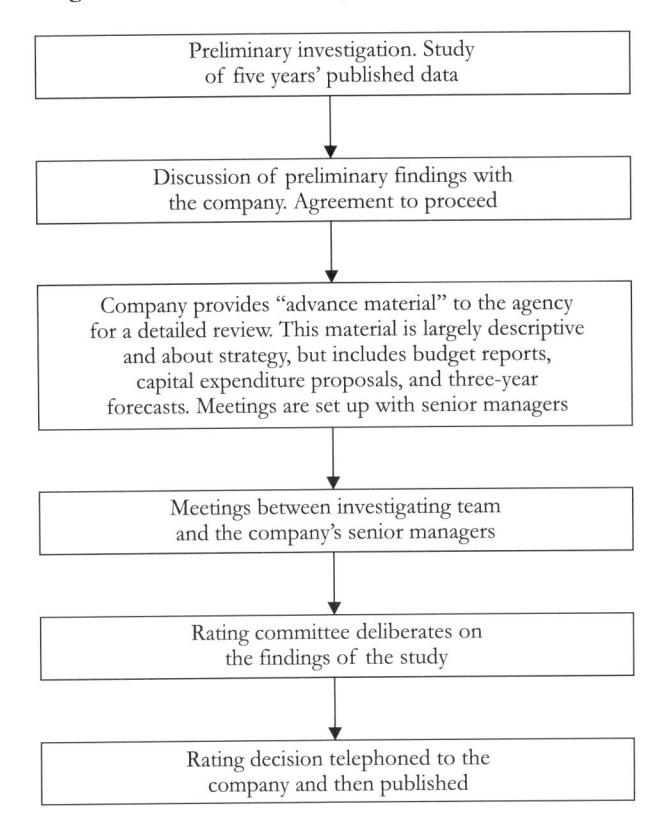

```
┌─────────────────────────────────────────┐
│   Preliminary investigation. Study      │
│      of five years' published data      │
└─────────────────────────────────────────┘
                    │
                    ▼
┌─────────────────────────────────────────┐
│  Discussion of preliminary findings with│
│   the company. Agreement to proceed     │
└─────────────────────────────────────────┘
                    │
                    ▼
┌─────────────────────────────────────────┐
│ Company provides "advance material" to  │
│ the agency for a detailed review. This  │
│ material is largely descriptive and     │
│ about strategy, but includes budget     │
│ reports, capital expenditure proposals, │
│ and three-year forecasts. Meetings are  │
│ set up with senior managers             │
└─────────────────────────────────────────┘
                    │
                    ▼
┌─────────────────────────────────────────┐
│  Meetings between investigating team    │
│  and the company's senior managers      │
└─────────────────────────────────────────┘
                    │
                    ▼
┌─────────────────────────────────────────┐
│    Rating committee deliberates on      │
│       the findings of the study         │
└─────────────────────────────────────────┘
                    │
                    ▼
┌─────────────────────────────────────────┐
│   Rating decision telephoned to the     │
│      company and then published         │
└─────────────────────────────────────────┘
```

In the detailed review for a company's credit rating, financial ratio analysis is an important issue. In addition, the business risk, industry risk and country risk of the company's operations are also investigated to obtain a longer-term view of the company's strengths and weaknesses. Standard & Poor's describes its framework for analysis as comprising two key components: "The first is oriented to business or competitive analysis; the second is related to financial analysis. It is critical to understand that the rating process is not limited to an examination of various financial measures. Proper assessment of debt protection levels requires a broader perspective, involving a thorough review of business fundamentals, including judgments about a company's competitive position and evaluation of management and its strategies."

The market share held by the company's products or services is often an important consideration in assessing its competitive position. The ability of an issuer to protect market share often can be inferred from its volume of long-term sales contracts, its new product developments, its backlog of confirmed orders, or by its ownership of a comprehensive distribution network. However, a large market share does not always give a market advantage or industry dominance.

Industry risk analysis is more general than product-market analysis. It considers the core strengths of the industry as a whole, its long-term prospects and the vulnerability of the industry to economic cycles. Industry features such as a history of labor unrest, government interference, the need for spending on capital equipment or R&D, also could be relevant.

Industry risk analysis sets an upper limit to a credit rating. A company with a very good competitive position in an industry in long-term decline such as steel, or in a cyclical business such as home-building, is unlikely to be given the highest credit rating.

Country risk analysis sometimes can be significant. The rating for a company based in a particular country normally will not be above the actual or implied debt rating for that country. Other factors in country risk analysis include state support for industry and whether the company is wholly or partly government owned.

As noted above, Aerospatiale the state-owned French aerospace and defense contractor, has been rated more highly by Standard & Poor's than purely financial considerations would have justified. On the other hand the Asian crisis that first came to prominence during 1997/98 could adversely affect the credit ratings of companies with major operations in the region.

Financial Ratio Analysis

Financial ratios often will set the boundaries for a credit rating, but are not used in themselves to fix a rating. There is certainly no formula for converting financial ratios into a credit rating. Standard & Poor's, for example, usually consider the following ratios to be significant.

For Assessing the Ability to Make Interest Payments on Time.
The operating profit (before deducting depreciation) as a percentage of sales. Depreciation is not deducted from profit because depreciation policies differ significantly between companies and can distort comparisons. Credit ratings depend largely on inter-company comparisons.

For property companies only, the *ratio of net rental income: gross interest cost* is used. If this ratio is below 1.0 times, it is unlikely that an investment grade credit rating will be given.

Fixed charge cover. This is the ratio of operating profits to fixed charges that the company must pay. Fixed charges are gross interest cost, contractual payments under operating leases and preference dividends. For an investment grade rating, Standard & Poor's take the view that a company must not be expected to pass a preference dividend, i.e. be at risk of an inability to pay dividend to preference shareholders.

For Assessing the Ability to Repay Debt Principal on Time
Cash flow is regarded as a better measure of a company's ability to repay its debts on time than its balance sheet structure. There is no fixed ideal minimum ratio for net cash flow to debt because different industries have different cash flow profiles. Compare, for example, highly liquid retailing companies with highly illiquid property companies. Retailing companies should have a much higher ratio of net cash inflow to debts than property companies because the cash cycle in retailing is faster and the need for retail companies to borrow in order to finance properties and other assets, should be much less. Key cash flow ratios are a cash flow to debt ratio and a cash flow interest cover.

Other Factors in the Assessment

Financial flexibility is also included in the credit rating assessment. Financial flexibility refers to a company's ability to raise additional finance, should it need to, from bank borrowings or issues of new debt or equity capital. The presence of non-core businesses or surplus assets with a substantial resale value might be significant also.

There are other items that a credit rating agency might wish to investigate if they appeared in a company's balance sheet. If anything is obscure and not properly explained, the rating agency will suspect the worst. Examples of such items are

- contingent liabilities, such as guarantees, legal cases outstanding, etc. These are amounts that the company could have to pay should a particular event occur; for example, there could be a contingent liability for $10 million in damages should the outcome of a court action be adverse
- off-balance-sheet finance and liabilities, such as property leases, contingent liabilities and pension obligations
- the practice of provision accounting and reserve accounting, widely used in some European countries such as France, Germany, and the UK. These are well-entrenched techniques of creative accounting
- the mix of debt capital according to maturity, fixed or floating rate basis and currency. A company with large amounts of debt in a hard currency that are maturing at around the same time could be a high credit risk.

Moody's Debt Ratings

Moody's use different categories to rate long-term and short-term debt, that is defined as senior debt with an original maturity of one year or less.

Moody's Short-Term Debt Ratings

There are three ratings for short-term debt, e.g. commercial paper, considered investment grade that indicate the relative ability of the debt issuer to repay. These are Prime 1, Prime 2 and Prime 3.

Moody's Short-Term Debt Ratings

Rating	Characteristics
Prime 1	Superior ability to repay. Assured sources of alternative liquidity. Leading position in a strong industry. High returns on capital employed. High ratio of equity finance. High level of profit cover for interest charges (interest cover). Strong cash generation.
Prime 2	Strong ability to repay. Ample sources of alternative liquidity. Similar characteristics to those of Prime 1, but to a lesser degree. More variability in profits growth, interest cover.
Prime 3	Acceptable ability to repay. Adequate sources of alternative liquidity. More affected by changes in industry and market condition. Variability in earnings could result in a requirement for relatively high borrowing and financial gearing.

Issuers of debt who do not fall into any of these categories are rated Not Prime, and are a higher credit/investment risk.

Moody's Long-Term Debt Ratings

Moody's use nine debt ratings for long-term debt, ranging from Aaa (triple A) down to C. Remember that ratings apply to the debt itself, but it is common to refer to companies and banks according to the rating given for their issued debt capital; for example, we might refer to a triple-A rated company.

Moody's Long-Term Debt Ratings

Rating	Characteristics
Aaa	Best quality bonds. Gilt-edged. Principal is secure. Interest payments are very well protected by large profits.
Aa	High-quality bonds, but not quite as high grade as Aaa, possibly because of greater variability in profit margins.
A	Bonds possess many favorable attributes and are medium to upper grade. Adequate security for principal and interest.
Baa	Medium-grade bonds, being neither highly protected nor poorly secured. Principal and interest are adequately secured at present, but some unreliability exists for the longer term. Some speculative characteristics as investments.

Ba	Bonds that are judged to have speculative characteristics as investments. Usually only a moderate protection of interest and principal.
B	Bonds that generally lack the attributes of a desirable investment. Protection of interest and principal over any long period of time is not well assured.
Caa	Bonds of poor standing, with some threat to security of principal or interest payments. Some such bonds might be in default already.
Ca	Bonds that are highly speculative. Often in default.
C	Lowest rating. Bonds have very poor prospects of ever achieving an investment (non-speculative) rating.

One of the features of Moody's ratings of banks is that if a subsidiary or branch of the bank issues debt obligations in one country, the debt rating for that branch will be the lower of the bank's own rating (parent company) or the sovereign rating for the country itself. For example, if an international bank with a triple-A rating issues debt obligations through a subsidiary in Australia, and if the sovereign rating of Australia is just Aa, the debt obligations of the bank's branch would be rated no higher than Aa.

Other Moody's Ratings

Other categories of ratings are applied to money market funds, insurance companies and preferred stock.

Standard & Poor's Credit Ratings

Like Moody's, Standard & Poor's is a credit rating agency that provides ratings for debt securities, or more exactly, for "the creditworthiness of an obliger with respect to a specific obligation". Sovereign ratings also are provided as assessments of a government's ability to meet its senior debt obligations punctually.

CREDIT RATING AGENCIES

Standard & Poor's Short-Term Ratings

A Standard & Poor's commercial paper rating is a current assessment of the likelihood of punctual payment of debt that has been issued with an original maturity of 12 months or less. The ratings are as follows

Standard & Poor's Short-Term Ratings

Rating	Characteristics
A-1	Highest category. Strong safety characteristics. An A-1+ rating indicates extremely strong safety characteristics.
A-2	Not as high as A-1, but still a satisfactory capacity for timely payments.
A-3	Adequate capacity for timely payments, but more vulnerable to adverse changes in circumstances than debt rated A-1 or A-2.
B	Only speculative capacity for timely payment.
C	Doubtful capacity for payment.
D	Payment is in default.

Standard & Poor's Long-Term Ratings

Ratings for long-term debt are grouped into two main categories

- investment grade ratings AAA, AA, A and BBB
- speculative grade ratings BB, B, CCC, CC, and C. A speculative grade rating indicates that the capacity of the debt issuer to meet interest payments and principal repayment is uncertain.

In addition, there are two further ratings: C1 and D.

Standard & Poor's Long-Term Debt Ratings

Ratings	Characteristics
Investment grades	
AAA	Highest rating. Capacity to make interest payments and principal repayment is extremely strong.
AA	Capacity to make interest payments and principal repayment is strong. Only marginally weaker than AAA grade.

33

A	Also a strong capacity to make interest payments and principal repayments, but with some susceptibility to adverse changes in circumstances and economic conditions.
BBB	Adequate capacity to make interest payments and principal repayments, but this capacity could be weakened by adverse changes in circumstances. Not as secure as other investment grade ratings.

Speculative grades

BB	Major continuing uncertainties or exposure to adverse changes in conditions could result in inadequate capacity to make timely payments of interest and principal. This rating is used for debt that is subordinated to senior debt with BBB- rating also.
B	Is currently able to meet interest payments and principal repayments, but a greater vulnerability to default than rating BB. This rating is used for debt that is subordinated to senior debt with a BB or BB- rating also.
CCC	Has a currently identified vulnerability to default, and is depending on favorable economic, business and financial conditions to avoid default. This rating is used for debt that is subordinated to senior debt with a B or B- rating also.
CC	Debt that is subordinated to senior debt with a CCC rating.
C	Debt that is subordinated to senior debt with a CCC- rating. Also used for debt where a bankruptcy petition has been filed but the debt is still being serviced.

Other grades

C1	Income bonds on which no interest is being paid.
D	Payment is in default, or a bankruptcy petition has been filed and default is likely.

Ratings AA to CCC might be modified by a plus (+) or minus (-) to indicate the relative standing of the debt within each rating category. Plus indicates a higher rating than minus.

It is common for debt issues to be rated by more than one agency. Standard & Poor's ratings should be broadly comparable to those of Moody's, although there have been instances where their views differ. For example, many of the rated companies in the aerospace sector enjoy a higher rating from Standard & Poor's than from Moody's. When the agencies differ in their views, there is a so-called split rating.

Fitch IBCA Ratings

Fitch IBCA Ltd is a UK credit rating agency that provides credit ratings on banks and the debt obligations of banks, as well as other companies.

The Fitch IBCA rating system for banks is designed to help users judge whether the bank would receive support if it ran into difficulties (a support rating) and assess its current performance (an individual rating).

Fitch IBCA Support Ratings

Support ratings assess the probability that a bank would receive support from the state or its shareholders in the event of financial difficulties. This has been a significant issue in the US, Sweden, Italy, and the UK with the well-publicized failures of Bank of Credit and Commerce International (BCCI) and Barings Bank.

Rating	Characteristics
1.	A bank for which there is a clear legal guarantee on the part of the state OR a bank of such importance both internationally and domestically that support from the state would be forthcoming if necessary. The state in question clearly must be prepared and able to support its principal banks.
2.	A bank for which state support would be forthcoming, even in the absence of a legal guarantee. For example, this could be because of the bank's importance to the economy or its historic relationships with the authorities.
3.	A bank or bank holding company that has institutional owners of sufficient reputation and possessing such resources that support would be forthcoming, if necessary.
4.	A bank for which support is likely but not certain.
5.	A bank, or bank holding company, for which support, although possible, cannot be relied upon.

Fitch IBCA Individual Ratings

Individual ratings assess how a bank would be viewed if it were entirely independent and could not rely on external support. These ratings are designed to assess a bank's exposure to, appetite for, and management of risk, and thus represent the likelihood that it would run into significant difficulties such that it would require support.

Rating	Characteristics of the bank
A	A very strong bank. Characteristics may include outstanding profitability and balance-sheet integrity, franchise, management, operating environment, or prospects.
B	A strong bank. There are no major concerns regarding the bank. Characteristics may include strong profitability and balance-sheet integrity, franchise, management, operating environment or prospects.
C	An adequate bank that possesses one or more troublesome aspects. There may be some concerns regarding its profitability and balance-sheet integrity, franchise, management, operating environment or prospects.
D	A bank that has weaknesses of internal and/or external origin. These are concerns regarding its profitability and balance-sheet integrity, franchise, management, operating environment or prospects.
E	A bank with very serious problems that either requires or is likely to require external support.

Users of Fitch IBCA ratings should make their own judgments about a bank from the support and individual ratings.

Fitch IBCA also has developed international credit ratings, long and short-term, that are applied to entities such as sovereign, banks and corporates and/or specific debt obligations. These are reproduced below. + or - may be added to a long- or short-term rating to denote relative status within major rating categories.

Fitch IBCA International Long-term Credit Ratings

Rating	Characteristic
Investment Grade	
AAA	Highest credit quality. AAA ratings denote the lowest expectation of credit risk. They are assigned only in cases of exceptionally strong capacity for timely payment of financial commitments. This capacity is highly unlikely to be adversely affected by foreseeable events.

AA	Very high credit quality. AA ratings denote a very low expectation of credit risk. They indicate very strong capacity for timely payment of financial commitments. This capacity is not significantly vulnerable to foreseeable events.
A	High credit quality. A ratings denote a low expectation of credit risk. The capacity for timely payment of financial commitments is considered strong. Nevertheless, this capacity may be more vulnerable to changes in circumstances or in economic conditions than is the case for higher ratings.
BBB	Good credit quality. BBB ratings indicate that currently there is a low expectation of credit risk. The capacity for timely payment of financial commitments is considered adequate, but adverse changes in circumstances and in economic conditions are more likely to impair this capacity. This is the lowest investment-grade category.

Speculative Grade

BB	Speculative. BB ratings indicate that there is a possibility of credit risk developing, particularly as the result of adverse economic change over time; however, business or financial alternatives may be available to allow financial commitments to be met. Securities rated in this category are not investment grade.
B	Highly speculative. B ratings indicate that significant credit risk is present, but a limited margin of safety remains. Financial commitments currently are being met; however, capacity for continued payment is contingent upon a sustained, favorable business and economic environment.
CCC, CC, C	High default risk. Default is a real possibility. Capacity for meeting financial commitments is solely reliant upon sustained, favorable business or economic developments. A CC rating indicates that default of some kind appears probable. C ratings signal imminent default.
DDD, DD and D	Default. Securities are extremely speculative, and their worth cannot exceed their recovery value in any liquidation or reorganization of the obligor. DDD designates the highest potential for recovery of amounts outstanding on any security involved. For US corporates, for example, DD indicates expected recovery of 50-90% of such outstandings, and D the lowest recovery potential, i.e. below 50%.

Fitch IBCA International Short-term Credit Ratings

Rating	Characteristics
F1	Highest credit quality. Indicates the strongest capacity for timely payment of financial commitments; may have an added + to denote any exceptionally strong credit feature.
F2	Good credit quality. A satisfactory capacity for timely payment of financial commitments, but the margin of safety is not as great as in the case of the higher ratings.
F3	Fair credit quality. The capacity for timely payment of financial commitments is adequate; however, near-term adverse changes could result in a reduction to non-investment grade.
B	Speculative. Minimal capacity for timely payment of financial commitments, plus vulnerability to near-term adverse changes in financial and economic conditions.
C	High default risk. Default is a real possibility. Capacity for meeting financial commitments is solely reliant upon a sustained, favorable business and economic environment.
D	Default. Denotes actual or imminent payment default.

Credit Watch

From time to time, a credit rating agency may reassess its rating for a particular debt issue, when circumstances have altered and there are greater doubts about the creditworthiness of the issuer. Before downgrading an issue to a lower credit rating, the agency could announce that it has put the rating under review, and might downgrade it in the near future. This is referred to as being put on credit watch, or in the case of the Fitch IBCA, rating watch.

When a debt issue is on credit watch, the rating agency will advise investors to use the rating with caution.

The Influence of Credit Rating Agencies

A credit rating will affect the interest rate at which organizations can borrow new funds – if at all – and is of direct relevance to credit risk assessment.

But the fact that the rating agencies failed to predict the far-east Asian crisis in late 1997, has resulted in some loss of confidence, especially among rating-sensitive investors.

The agencies downgraded the most troubled Asian countries' ratings between January and March 1998, South Korea, Indonesia, Thailand and Malaysia, after the seriousness of the problems had come to light.

The confidence problem was exacerbated by the agencies putting the eastern bloc countries on Credit Watch for a downgrade following the far-east Asian crisis. They were accused of being overly cautious, reactive rather than proactive, and aching to catch up with the market, rather than leading the market.

Do Ratings from Agencies Ever Differ?

Credit ratings are based on analysts' judgments. Therefore a rating by Standard & Poor's occasionally can differ from a rating for the same issue by Moody's.

Example
In 1992, concern about the financial position of the three major Swiss banks made both Standard & Poor's and Moody's review their ratings. Standard & Poor's confirmed its triple-A rating of all three banks (Union Bank of Switzerland, Crédit Suisse and Swiss Bank Corporation). Moody's, however, downgraded the rating of two of the banks, leaving just UBS among the three with a triple-A rating.

Some difference of opinion was still in evidence in June 1998, Standard & Poor's gave Swiss Bank Corporation and UBS an AA+ rating, and

Moody's gave the same banks a triple-A rating. The newly combined entity was still to be rated at this time.

Summary

The purpose of a credit rating is to give investors a guide as to the likelihood of receiving interest and principal repayments on schedule from that investment. However, in view of the track record of the credit rating agencies, and the depth of their analysis of the organization, ratings are used by other companies and banks for the purpose of setting general credit limits for the organization.

It is the debt issuer, rather than the investor or lender that must ask for a debt issue to be rated. Many investors will refuse to invest in an organization's debt capital unless the debt has a credit rating. Investor pressures therefore force organizations to ask for a rating whenever they plan a major new debt issue. This probably has helped to enhance the status of credit ratings, and secure their widespread use by banks and companies as well as by investment institutions.

The major limitation of credit ratings is that they are confined to large organizations. Credit managers looking for external assessments on smaller companies have to rely to other information sources, such as credit bureaus.

External Information Sources

When a customer applies for credit for the first time, the credit manager's task is to decide whether to agree to open an account for the customer and if so, what the credit limit and terms should be.

The purpose of credit information is to give the provider of credit some reassurance that the amount owed will be paid in full and on time. The credit manager needs to decide

- for how long credit can be granted, i.e. for how long can the customer hold on to the money that he owes, and
- what amount can be risked as a potential bad debt, i.e. how much credit should be given without creating an over-exposure to risk.

These are the two key points that a standard terms-of-credit letter ought to contain.

An example is shown on the facing page.

The credit manager could give credit terms without carrying out a check on the customer, but the exposure to credit risk from this do-nothing approach could be extremely high. More likely, the manager will seek information on which to base a judgment.

Reference to a credit bureau or credit reference agency, or to other credit information sources is a commonly used option.

Our Ref: A/C 12345432

Alpha Inc
Beta Block
Fifty-Second Street
Washington DC
10634

16th August 1999

<u>Attn:</u> Mr. J. P. Griers

Dear Sirs

Re: Your credit account with Tango Inc

We note from our sales ledger records that your company has recently made a request to Tango Inc for goods or services to be supplied on a credit basis. A credit facility of $11,000 has been set up initially and this can be reviewed at a later date if you so require.

May we draw your attention to our terms of trading that require payment of our invoices within 21 days of the date of our invoice, unless otherwise agreed in writing with Tango Inc.

We look forward to a long and mutually profitable business relationship between our organizations, and if you have any queries or comments regarding the operation of your trading account would you please contact the undersigned.

Yours faithfully

**T Merriman
Credit Controller**

Credit Bureaus

Credit bureaus provide information about companies, or partnerships and sole traders that can be used to assess creditworthiness. However, bureaus differ in the services they offer to clients. Some simply supply historical accounting records about the company under investigation. Copies of annual accounts for the past two or three years can be delivered by post, possibly within 48 hours.

Large bureaus can provide on-line information to a client, so that the client can make an immediate credit decision. Some bureaus offer their own credit assessment or rating on the accounts of companies. Major credit reference agencies include Equifax, Dun & Bradstreet and Experian.

Why Use a Bureau?

The purpose of using a bureau is to obtain extra information that will help decide what credit terms to offer to a customer. Information can be sought about potential new customers, about whom nothing is known. For existing customers, a bureau can supply new information about a business that could affect its credit standing.

In contrast to credit rating agencies that assess large organizations, bureaus can provide information about small businesses. Their services are therefore relevant to the day-to-day tasks of routine credit management in all sizes of company.

Credit risk stems from fraud as well as financial weakness. When an account is opened for an unknown customer, the credit manager's concerns are not just that the customer won't be able to pay, but also that the customer could deliberately intend not to pay for goods or services obtained on credit. Information from a bureau occasionally can help alert a credit manager to the possibility of a fraudulent customer.

Much of the information available to an agency is published or exists as public information, such as company accounts. This information could be accessed directly by a credit manager. However, agencies have particular strengths that can justify the use of their services.

- They have built up a huge database of credit information that is kept up-to-date.
- They know where to obtain relevant information, e.g. about company liquidations.

- They could have access to information about a company's payment records, or to other trade reference information supplied by their clients. This information could be of particular value to other clients.
- They also can obtain information directly. A letter could be sent to a company or partnership, etc., on behalf of, and with the knowledge of, a client who has asked for a credit report, asking for answers to particular questions. A bureau has the experience and skills to ask relevant questions and to judge the replies.

Credit Bureau Reports

The type of report that a bureau or credit information agency provides differs from agency to agency. Large agencies offer a variety of reports.

A report could be limited to giving information about the capital structure of the company, its registered office, directors' names and addresses, plus, if available, a list of stockholders and a copy of the company's latest accounts.

A status report gives up-to-date financial information about a business, extracted from the database of the bureau. These reports include records of any hire purchase defaults and court judgments against the business. Status reports can be supplemented by an ongoing update service that provides new information about the business as soon as it is collected.

Some agencies consist of member organizations that grant credit to their customers as part of their normal trading operations. Records are maintained of credits granted to customers by each of the agency's members, and of bad debts that members have suffered, and bankruptcies, insolvencies, or unsatisfied court judgments involving their customers. An agency member, before deciding whether to grant credit to a customer, can check with the agency to establish whether there is anything on record about the customer's credit history. The agency will be able to provide a status report based on its knowledge of specific credit transactions by that customer.

Dun & Bradstreet is one of the most well-known credit reference agencies, with offices throughout the world. A major strength of Dun & Bradstreet's services is its very large payment profile data bank that contains information about payments records of companies and other businesses. This information is obtained from clients and fed into Dun & Bradstreet's database at regular intervals.

A payment score report can be obtained from this data. This is a numerical score that rates a company's performance in paying its bills. It is based on an analysis of payment records on the agency's database. Actual payments are compared with the credit terms that were offered for each recorded transaction, e.g. end of month, one month from invoice date, net 14 days, 2% settlement discount on seven days, net 30 days, etc. On the scale of 100 down to 0, 100 represents a company that regularly pays in advance of the due date, 90 represents a company that regularly takes early settlement discounts, 80 represents a prompt payer and 30 a company that takes on average around three months beyond the due date.

An agency also could have a credit rating system whereby it gives its own credit rating to companies. A list of these ratings would be made available to the agency's clients.

Choosing a Bureau

There are many other credit reference agencies each with its own particular sources of information and approach to credit assessment and credit reporting.

Reports can be provided in hard copy format or on-line, according to the client's preference. The charges to the client vary according to the nature of the service provided.

For a corporate credit controller seeking information to help with a credit decision, it might be appropriate to ask two or more bureaus for reports that can be compared. Credit managers certainly should be aware of the services available from different agencies, and at what price, and then select the service and the agency that best suits their requirements.

By telephoning a few agencies to find out what credit reports or credit ratings they can provide, and at what cost, a credit controller using an agency for the first time should be able to decide which agency or agencies to use.

Trade References and Bank Status Reports

For a credit controller who doesn't want to use an agency to obtain credit information about an unknown customer, there are other options

- asking for trade references from a potential new customer, and/or
- asking for trade references from a potential new customer, and/or
- asking for a bank status report.

The potential customer can be asked to give the names and addresses of two existing suppliers who would be able to give a trade reference, indicating that the customer is reliable and has a history of prompt payments. These references should be chased up, and letters sent out promptly to the referees, with documentation to show that the customer has consented to the reference being sought.

Bank status reports can be sought from the potential customer's bank. This report is a banker's opinion about the customer. The protocol is for a company to ask for a report through its own bank, with an indication of the amount of credit envisaged. For example, is the customer's creditworthiness sufficiently good to justify a credit limit of $5,000? The bank will then pass on the request to the potential customer's bank that prepares the status report.

Summary

Small businesses often lack the in-house financial skills to do their own credit analysis. These would be well advised to take credit references on all new customers and update them regularly.

However, credit information from external sources can provide only comfort, or warnings, to the credit controller. The final decision is the credit controller's own, based on facts, judgment and an evaluation of the credit risk.

Inhouse Credit Assessments

In addition to, or instead of, using credit information from external agencies, a company can establish a system for the assessment of customers by inhouse analysts. Banks do most of their credit analysis work inhouse. Companies can use a team of analysts, or the credit manager, depending on the size of the company and its business, to assess trade customers. Very large companies can regularly assess their banks.

Methods of Corporate Credit Risk Analysis

The most common form of credit risk assessment on companies is a financial analysis. This involves studying the available financial information about the company, drawn perhaps from its annual report and accounts. A number of different financial ratios can be calculated, and the ratios can provide some indications about the company's profitability, capital strength, liquidity and control over working capital. The adequacy of cash flows also can be assessed.

The techniques of financial ratio analysis are the subject of *Corporate Credit Analysis*, a separate title in this series.

In addition to financial ratio analysis, however, other methods of assessment can be used. These are complementary techniques, and should be used in addition to analyzing a company's accounts. However, they are probably unreliable guides to credit risk if used on their own. Such methods include

- collecting information about the company from newspapers, journals and other sources, to build up a company profile
- credit scoring
- profit or cash flow projections.

Building Up a Company Profile

The activities of some companies, particularly public companies, are more widely reported than those of others. Stock market information about public companies is reported daily in the press, showing share price movements and the current market capitalization of the company. For the largest companies, there is information about the volume of stocks traded daily. Reasons for a significant rise or fall in a share price are also usually reported.

Newspapers and journals often feature articles about the performance or current concerns of companies. Occasionally published information can provide useful insights into a company's financial problems.

Share Price

A very large fall in the share price of a company could be a prelude to its financial collapse. Large public companies whose share price has slumped will often attract regular press comment. Some companies are able to recover from these difficulties; many do not. Suppliers and banks could decide to limit the amount of credit they are prepared to give to companies in these difficulties unless and until there is a recovery in the share price and the trading outlook.

Dividend Cover

Dividends are important to investors in stocks so public companies in some countries try to maintain or increase their dividends to stockholders each year from one year to the next. When a company's profits have slumped, its ability to pay dividends out of current profits could be at risk, unless dividends are cut as well.

During prosperous years, many public companies are able to maintain a ratio of profits to dividends of about 2.5:1, or 2.5 times. This ratio is termed the dividend cover ratio. For example, if a company's annual profits after tax are $10 million and dividends declared for the year are $4 million, the dividend would be covered 2.5 times by profits, i.e. the dividend cover is 2.5:1, or 10:4. The profits not distributed as dividends are retained in the business for reinvestment.

If profits fall, however, but dividends are maintained at the same level, the dividend cover will also fall. In a recession, some companies could pay an uncovered dividend, i.e. a dividend higher than the current year's profits. When the dividend cover is low, cash flows and liquidity could come under strain because dividend payments would take much-needed cash out of the company.

Example
Alpha's profits after tax in Year 1 were $5 million. Its dividends for the Year 1 were $4 million. In Year 2, profits fell to $2.4 million, but the dividends were maintained at $4 million.

Analysis
In Year 1, the dividend cover was just 1.25 times (5:4). The company retained profits of just $1 million to reinvest in the business. If Alpha has a large program of new capital expenditures, it would probably need extra funding from other sources. In Year 2, the dividend cover falls below 1.0 to 0.6 times (2.4:4). Dividend payments will exceed profits by $1.6 million, and Alpha will have to obtain the cash from elsewhere.

Unless profits improve in Year 3, or the dividend is cut, Alpha's cash problems will intensify over time.

Other Information

Information about companies and their directors can be gathered from a variety of sources to help credit managers build up a profile of a company. Published information is restricted mainly to large companies. On the fairly rare occasions when such companies attract adverse publicity, banks and suppliers can reassess its credit status.

Credit Scoring

Credit scoring is a method of credit assessment that uses statistical techniques, based perhaps on financial ratio analysis, for measuring the likelihood or probability that an applicant for credit will pay or repay in full and on time.

Banks have developed their own credit-scoring systems that they might use to assess customers. Details of their scoring methods are not made public, but it is useful to look at these systems in general detail.

A credit-scoring system is based on identifying the key attributes of an applicant for credit, to which weightings or points can be applied to derive a credit score. For a business, attributes might include sales turnover, profitability, the number of its employees, the nature of its business operations, the number of years since the business was established, its location and so on. Alternatively, they might be financial ratios, calculated from the company's accounts. Key attributes are those for which there is a statistically significant correlation with the likelihood that the applicant will repay the credit in full and on time.

A proper credit-scoring system is one that is statistically sound, demonstrably reliable and regularly validated. It should have a high level of predictive ability in distinguishing between credit applicants who will repay punctually and those who will not. A system is designed to predict what proportion of customer accounts that have scores within a given score range will perform acceptably.

The lender can establish cut-off scores for the system. A cut-off score will be used

- to say yes or no to a request for credit based on the likelihood that the applicant will not repay punctually, or
- to set credit limits. For a given credit score, total credit facilities would not be allowed to exceed a certain limit.

The cut-off scores that a lender establishes are likely to be varied up or down according to the lender's financial situation and ability to provide credit finance.

Behavioral scoring is a form of credit scoring that can be applied to a lender's existing customers. The attributes that are scored relate to the customer's behavior in servicing his account, such as the proportion of payments that are late. Decisions to renew credit facilities or to increase a customer's credit limit will be made according to the customer's credit score.

Cash flow Projections

As part of its credit analysis procedures, a bank could attempt to prepare a cash flow projection for a company. Its purpose would be to estimate the company's future cash flows from trading operations, and to assess whether these are likely to be sufficient to pay interest, tax and dividends, and to either repay the loan principal or keep its overdraft within a prescribed limit.

The preparation of cash forecasts is described in much more detail in *Cash Flow Management*, another series in the Financial Risk Management program. Here, just a few points will be made about how the task could be approached.

Cash flow projections will vary in their detail and sophistication. Some will be prepared by customers and presented to the bank as part of an application procedure for borrowing. Others will be prepared entirely by the bank.

A cash flow projection can be constructed using a simple standard model or template, and guidelines can be provided to instruct the forecaster in the step-by-step procedures. A simple format is shown opposite.

Cash flow Projection

	Illustrative Figures
	$000
Sales	20,000
Cost of sales	-12,000
Gross incomet	8,000
Distribution costs	-2,500
Administrative costs	-3,000
Other items	0
Income before interest and taxation	2,500
Add back depreciation	1,700
Operational cash flows	4,200
Working capital changes	
(Increase)/decrease in stocks	-800
(Increase)/decrease in debtors	-900
Increase/(decrease) in creditors	600
Cash flow from operations after working capital adjustments	3,100
Interest payments	-1,100
	2,000
Taxation payments	-500
Cash flow for capital expenditure, loan repayments and dividends	1,500

There will be a small number of key variables, or cash drivers, for any business. These are likely to be

- Sales
- Cost of sales, as a percentage of sales value
- Distribution costs and administrative expenses, as a percentage of sales value
- Working capital management, the management of stocks, debtors and creditors
- Tax payments
- Interest rates
- Dividend payout ratio, i.e. the proportion of profits paid as dividends
- Capital expenditure

Assumptions have to be made for all of these variables. The projection should be prepared using cautious assumptions. Revenue should not be overstated nor costs understated. Almost inevitably there will be a high margin of error in the projections, even when the bank has access to the company's own cash flow assumptions and projections.

The starting point for constructing a cash flow projection should be an estimate of sales over the forecast period. Sales turnover is the key estimate, even though it is usually difficult to forecast with confidence. Having made an estimate for sales, assumptions can then be made about costs to calculate an operational profit for the forecast period.

Cost of sales. The cost of sales could be estimated as a fixed percentage of the sales figure. This percentage could be based on the company's most recent accounts. For example, if last year a company's sales were $1 million and its cost of sales were $400,000, the cost of sales as a percentage of sales turnover would be 40%. If projected sales are forecast at $1.1 million, the projected cost of sales, based on an assumption that this will be 40% of turnover, would be $440,000 (40% of $1.1 million).

Gross income is the difference between sales and the cost of sales. It can be measured as a percentage of the sales figure also.

Income before interest and taxation is the gross profit minus distribution costs and administrative costs, plus or minus any other items.

Distribution costs and administrative costs. It could be sufficient to make the assumption that these costs do not change from one year to the next. They can then be estimated by taking the amount in the company's most recent accounts, adjusted for any anticipated cost inflation. Alternatively, these costs could be estimated as a fixed percentage of sales turnover.

Other items should be included only if significant, such as interest or dividends likely to be received from investments.

Profits and cash flows are not the same. If a company makes profits of $500,000, it should not expect money in the bank to increase by the same amount. One reason for the difference between profit and cash flow is that some costs that are charged against profits are notional costs that do not represent a cash payment. The most significant of these costs is amortization. This is a notional cost to spread the cost of a fixed asset over the years of its expected use, and does not represent an item of cash expenditure. The cash expenditure would have been incurred when the fixed assets were purchased.

In order to estimate cash flows from income, notional costs such as amortization should be added back to the income figure. A figure for amortization can be based on the amortization charge in the company's most recent accounts. Income plus amortization gives a value that could be described as operational cash flows.

Working capital changes. Income and cash flows can differ because of changes over the forecast period in the amount of working capital, particularly in stocks, debtors and creditors. Purchases of stock use up cash. An increase in stock levels indicates that purchases have exceeded consumption of stock in the period, and that cash payments for stock have therefore exceeded the cost of stock sold in the period.

Similarly, debtors represent customers to whom goods or services have been sold, but payment is still due. The existence of a debtor indicates that there has been a sale at a profit. The profit has been earned, but the cash has not yet been received. An increase in debtors means that cash receipts from sales will be less than the amount of sales, and that cash flow therefore will be lower than income.

Cash flow Adjustments

Cash flows less than income when	Cash flows more than income when
stock levels increase	stock levels fall
the amount of debtors increases	the amount of debtors falls
the amount of creditors falls	the amount of creditors increases

Adjustments to cash flows for working capital changes are required only when changes in working capital can be anticipated. A reasonable assumption is that stocks, debtors and creditors will increase or fall in proportion to the anticipated increase or decline in annual sales turnover. If a rise or fall in sales turnover has been assumed, normally it would be appropriate to make an allied assumption about any changes in working capital.

Example
Last year Beta had sales turnover of $1 million, and end-of-year stocks of $100,000, debtors of $200,000 and creditors of $150,000. It is anticipated that sales next year will fall by 10% to $900,000.

Analysis
It can be assumed that stocks, debtors and creditors will all fall by 10%. The effect on cash flows would be as follows:

	Effect on cash flows $
Reduction in stocks (10% of $100,000)	+10,000
Fall in debtors (10% of $200,000)	+20,000
Fall in creditors (10% of $150,000)	-15,000
	+15,000

The cash flow projection can be completed by producing estimates for interest payments based on the company's estimated debts and an assumption about the rate of interest, and taxation, perhaps taken as a percentage of operational cash flow or income before interest.

The resulting figure, that could be negative but normally should be a positive value, is the amount of cash that the company should be capable of generating, after paying interest charges. This cash would be available for capital expenditures, dividends and for the repayment of loan principal.

The bank can then assess whether this surplus cash is likely to be adequate, or whether the company could be forced to rely on additional funding for its capital expenditures. A negative cash flow, with cash payments excluding receipts, would indicate an inability to pay interest charges, and suggest an unacceptable credit risk.

Example
Gamma's financial results last year were as follows

	$
Sales	6,000,000
Cost of sales	3,000,000
Gross income	3,000,000
Distribution costs	-1,500,000
Administrative expenses	-500,000
Income before interest and tax	1,000,000
Interest charges	-800,000
Income before tax	200,000
Taxation	-60,000
Net Income	140,000
Dividends	100,000
Retained income	40,000

Gamma expects to increase sales next year by 10%, but would need a loan of $250,000 for new capital expenditure. The interest cost on this loan would be 12%.

Gamma had stock in hand of $500,000 at the end of last year, debtors of $800,000 and creditors of $300,000. The depreciation charge last year was $75,000.

Gamma's bank liaison officer wishes to prepare a cash flow projection for the company as part of an assessment of the loan application.

Analysis
Bank officers have to decide what assumptions to make, using their best judgment. The selected assumptions could be as follows

Item	Assumption
Cost of sales	Same percentage of sales as last year (50%)
Gross income	Same percentage of sales as last year (50%)
Distribution costs	Increase by same percentage as the increase in sales (+10%)
Administrative costs	Same as last year

Depreciation	Same as last year ($75,000) plus $25,000 to allow for depreciation on new capital assets purchased	
Stocks	Increase by 10%, the same rate of increase as for sales turnover	
Debtors	Increase by 10%	
Creditors	Increase by 10%	
Interest	Same as last year, plus 12% interest on new loan of $250,000	
Taxation	Assume that the rate of taxation, as a percentage of profits before tax, will be the same as last year. This was 30% (60,000 ÷ 200,000)	
Dividend	Same as last year	

Gamma: Cash flow Projection for the Next year

	$	Comment
Sales	6,600,000	(+10%)
Cost of sales	-3,300,000	(50% of sales)
Gross income	3,300,000	(50% of sales)
Distribution costs	-1,650,000	($1,500,000 plus 10%)
Administrative costs	-500,000	(same as last year)
Income before interest and taxation	1,150,000	
Add back depreciation	100,000	($75,000 + $25,000)
Operational cash flow	1,250,000	
Working capital changes		
Increase in stocks	-50,000	(10% of $500,000)
Increase in debtors	-80,000	(10% of $800,000)
Increase in creditors	+30,000	(10% of $300,000)
Cash flow from operations after working capital adjustments	1,150,000	
Interest payments	-830,000	(last year's $800,000 plus 12% of $250,000)
	320,000	
Taxation payments	-96,000	(Income after interest but before tax = $1,150,000-$830,000

		= $320,000
		Tax = 30% of £320,000)
Cash surplus before dividends	224,000	
Dividends	-100,000	
Cash surplus	124,000	

These assumptions would produce the cash flow projection above. This projection suggests that Gamma could have sufficient cash flows to support the cost of the loan. However, any capital expenditures in addition to the $250,000 financed by the loan should be considered. The cash surplus after dividends is not much in excess of $100,000. The bank officer might wish to take her cash flow projection into subsequent years, to assess what Gamma's longer-term liquidity might be.

Summary

Inhouse credit assessments of companies are based largely on financial ratio analysis. However, other techniques can be used to contribute towards the credit analyst's assessment. These include monitoring reports about the company in the national press or trade journals. Press reports are insufficient on their own for a full credit assessment, but can provide valuable supplementary information. Cash flow projections are a form of financial analysis but do not involve an in-depth evaluation of a company's financial ratios and are often based on fairly simple assumptions. Although not fully reliable for this reason, cash flow projections can be a useful supplement to ratio analysis, particularly for bankers.

Industry Risk and Country Risk

A credit manager or banker should take into account the immediate financial circumstances of the customer's business, and also the economic and environmental factors, that usually are outside the customer's control, of the industry and country within which the customer operates.

Industry Risk

Industry risk arises from the possibility that an industry could go into decline or recession, and the consequences if either were to happen. If either happened, a consequence would be that a large number of companies within the industry would fail. For a company or bank with a large portfolio of customers in the industry, there could be a serious credit risk from a large increase in bad debts and late payments among that group of customers. The risk is probably greatest in industries that go through cycles of decline, recovery and growth, because at some time in the future, if it isn't already happening in the present, a period of decline will be inevitable.

A recession also causes more acute problems in certain sectors as industries move through the economic cycle. Certain industries are said to have a volatile revenue dynamic in that sales volume is directly related to the economic cycle and will rise and fall according to the position of the cycle. When coupled with relatively high levels of fixed costs, this leads to high levels of business failure. Examples of sectors susceptible to these trends include property and construction, entertainment and tourism, hotels, restaurants and airlines.

Obtaining Information for Industry Analysis

A supplier or bank should know which industry each customer is in and who are the competitors or market leaders. Information about an industry can be gathered from a number of sources. Some industries are well documented by large credit reference agencies, such as Dun & Bradstreet.

Major industries are the subject of continual review by analysts. Industrial sector reports by stock market analysts are no longer as common as they once were, but still can be obtained.

Industrial reports and market surveys are sometimes available from publishers. Often these deal with international markets, such as the world waste paper industry. However, a note of caution, when using such reports it is important to consider just how reliable and independent they are.

When a company or a bank has considerable exposure to a particular industry, it is advisable to subscribe to relevant trade magazines. Usually the customer will advise which magazines are most appropriate.

Where detailed industry data is not available for comparative purposes, the annual report and accounts of competitor firms should be obtained and thoroughly reviewed.

Country Risk

Country risk arises from the potential consequences of changes in the conditions within a particular country or group of countries. In the context of credit management, it is the risk of bad debts from customers in that country, or late payments as a consequence of events or developments outside the customer's own control.

Country risk can be caused by

- political risk
- economic risk
- currency risk
- regulatory risk.

Political risk is the threat from changes in the country's government and government policy. There could be a threat of invasion, e.g. Kuwait in 1990, civil war, e.g. in the former Yugoslavia, or terrorism. Sometimes, the possibility of a radical change in government could be a concern; for example, exporters from western countries could be concerned about a fundamentalist Islamic government taking control in Algeria. Credit risk also can come from less dramatic political change, such as a decision by the government to end its guarantees of payment for the debts of state-owned industries.

Economic risk arises from the prospects of deteriorating economic conditions within a country, or the consequences of existing poor conditions. Economic risk can arise from

- the prospect of an economic depression
- the decline of particular industries in the country
- high rates of inflation
- the prospect of industrial unrest
- the possibility or existence of exchange controls
- nationalization or privatization of industries, and the possible consequences.

Currency risk is a factor associated with economic risk. This is the risk losses from an adverse movement in exchange rates.

Example 1
Alpha exports large quantities of goods on credit to Finland. Goods are invoiced in dollars. The Finnish markka falls by 10% in value against the dollar over a period of about a month.

Analysis
Customers in Finland will have to pay 10% more to settle their debts to Alpha unless they have hedged their currency exposure. There could be an increased risk to Alpha of bad debts or late payments.

Example 2
In November 1997 the South Korean government sought a rescue package from the International Monetary Fund in the form of standby loans totalling $20 billion to avoid defaulting on short-term foreign debts and to replenish dwindling currency reserves after a run on the won.

Regulatory risk is the risk of losses because of regulations or legal procedures in a particular country. Customers could use the legal system in their country to avoid or delay payment to foreign suppliers, forcing the supplier to seek payment through an unfamiliar procedure. Many companies that export to potentially high-risk countries are likely to insist on a secure method of payment, such as a confirmed letter of credit.

Customs and habits in a particular country also can be significant for credit risk. Late payment, for example, is common business practice in Italy. Therefore exporters to Italy should be aware that credit terms can be disregarded, and should make sure that they have sufficient funds to support a large volume of Italian debtors.

Assessing Country Risk

Country risk is well recognized by investment managers, who must make decisions about whether or not to invest in bond issues by governments or by large organizations in a particular country. When country risk is high, the risks of investing in these issues could be unacceptable.

To an investment manager, the major element in country risk is economic risk. If the country's currency falls in value because of a deteriorating national economy, the value of any investment in that country also would decline.

Specialist companies can provide country risk analysis reports. These focus largely on prospects for the country's economy, focusing on key ratios that measure economic strength. For example

- the ratio of net imports to foreign currency reserves
- the size of interest payments on the country's foreign debts in relation to the volume of the country's exports

- the size of the national debt in relation to the size of the country's annual gross domestic product
- the increase or decrease in foreign currency reserves
- the percentage growth or decline in exports.

Country risk analysis of this type is quite specialized, and focuses on long-term risk.

Banks and exporters are interested in the ability of specific customers to pay what they owe on time. Long-term economic prospects can have some relevance, but credit managers are mostly interested in a different type of information. They want to assess whether conditions in a country might change, so that a customer will be unable to pay or be given an excuse for not paying. These changes could arise directly from political events, new laws or regulations, a sharp movement in the exchange rate, labor unrest, etc. These are more specific project risk items.

Banks that lend abroad and exporting companies should monitor these events by collecting information from as many sources as possible. Published sources include newspaper and trade magazine articles, television reports, and the internet. Discussions with colleagues, including those in competitor organizations, can provide useful background information.

How is the Information Used?

To keep credit risk under control, consideration could be given to whether a total credit limit ought to be set for customers in a particular industry or country. A policy for limiting credit could be set by the board of directors, and applied at an operational level.

Risk and Banks
Banks in particular should be aware of industry risks, because their loan exposures can be very high.

A criticism of many lending banks in the past has been their apparent failure to monitor industry risk until the industry falls into recession, and bad debts have already been incurred.

In years of economic growth and optimism banks have lent, perhaps without adequate credit protection. When there are many potentially successful businesses wanting to borrow, it can be tempting for banks to lend freely in order to maintain market share, especially when specific industries such as property and construction, are attracting large amounts of new loans. The result is the classic consequence of supply exceeding demand with downward pressure on both price and quality.

When bad debts subsequently occur, the risks of over-exposure to a particular industry or country become apparent too late. Banks can then withdraw from lending to whole sectors of industry or to all customers in a particular country. Alternatively, acceptance criteria for new loans become tougher.

Risk and Companies
Not all companies set limits on their credit exposures to particular industries or countries. Credit managers could be given authority to grant credit at their discretion, perhaps within an overall control limit.

However, if a company gives credit to a large number of customers in the same industry, its management ought to consider how much credit it can safely give them in total. In the event of downturn in the industry, a company should wish to avoid being brought to financial collapse by the difficulties of its customers.

This does not necessarily require a formal system of monitoring. Many credit managers are only too well aware of the problems and risks of selling on credit to customers in particular parts of the world or particular industries.

For example, many companies are reluctant to sell large value items to customers in some industries and in countries without a secure method of payment, e.g. payment in advance, or payment by confirmed letter of credit, or without arranging credit insurance.

Example 1
Gamma is a large printing company. Its customers can be divided into four broad groups according to the type of printing they buy: books, magazines, brochures and other work. Gamma's management is aware that falling advertising revenues have created problems for magazine publishers, who are now taking longer to pay. Several magazine customers have asked for more credit.

Analysis
The decision whether or not to give more credit to these customers can be taken with some understanding of the current difficulties in the magazine publishing business. Gamma's credit manager could discuss these problems, and concerns about late payments, before reaching a decision. It could be advisable for Gamma to set a limit on the total credit it allows to magazine customers.

Credit Limits for Regions of the World

Credit limits also could be set for high-risk regions of the world, such as Latin America, central and eastern Europe and the Balkan countries, parts of Africa and Asia. The perceived risk of each region could vary over time, and credit limits, as for individual countries, can be reviewed on a regular basis.

One of the most dramatic instances of downgrading the rating of a sovereign borrower was that of South Korea. In October 1997 it had the same credit rating as Sweden and Italy; by January 1998 it had been downgraded to junk-bond status.

The South Korean case is significant because many western institutional investors are barred from investing in countries that do not have investment-grade status.

Credit limits for regions of the world should be complementary to country limits because the sum of the parts can build up to an over-risky whole. For example, if there are four countries in one particular region, and a company sets total trade credit limits of $100 million to customers in each of those countries, these limits might be satisfactory for each country taken individually. However, on a regional view, total credit of $400 million for the four countries might seem excessive. Credit limits therefore could be set at $100 million for each country, subject to an overall limit of perhaps $300 million for the region as a whole.

Credit Limits for Currency Blocs

Volatility in exchange rates could affect the creditworthiness of overseas customers by increasing the costs to them of buying a company's goods. For example, suppose that a company sells goods priced in dollars to customers in the EU, and annual sales are £100 million. If the exchange rate were to change from 60p = $1 to 50p = $1, the costs to customers would rise by 20% from $60 million to $72 million. This large increase in price could result in fewer annual sales and also in more bad debts, because some customers would be unable to pay their debts unless they had hedged their exposure to the risk in the foreign exchange markets.

Summary

Banks, and companies, should monitor the risks of giving credit to both particular industries and particular countries. This monitoring process can be more significant in the years of growth and prosperity. Credit managers should then be pessimistic, and consider the potential consequences of any downturn in the industry or the country's economy. This can help banks and companies either to set credit limits or insist on other forms of credit protection, such as credit insurance.

To apply credit limits to customers in an industry or a country, it is important to have a system for collecting and analyzing relevant information. Credit managers should remain aware of what is going on and be alert to the signs of economic downturn.

The Assessment of Banks

An aspect of credit management that has not received the attention it deserves, is the policy of a company towards its bank or banks.

What is the Credit Risk with Banks?

Banks can be a credit risk for companies that deal with them. Perhaps the obvious credit risk is that if a bank were to go into liquidation depositors would lose their money. In the extreme, if a bank goes into liquidation, the borrowing company could face a call from the liquidator for the immediate repayment of a loan. The need to find an alternative source of funds at very short notice would almost certainly force the company to pay more to get them. The Bank of New England failed in 1991, having for the previous few years offered competitive prices on its loans in the form of low commitment fees to attract big UK multinationals. Any company that relied on this bank for much of its credit would almost certainly have faced immediate collapse as its credit facilities were suddenly withdrawn.

The sudden closure of a bank and the threat of lost deposits might still seem a remote and unlikely event. However, the closure of the Bank of Credit and Commerce International (BCCI) in July 1991 should still send a warning.

In 1992, the Swedish banking sector ran into financial difficulties. Bad debts on loans were high and property prices had collapsed, affecting the value of the banks' security on bad loans. In addition, in autumn 1992

Swedish interest rates were raised to record high levels to protect the krone, decimating the demand for loans from customers. Even in October, the central bank's discount rate was still at 50%. The Swedish banks as a whole became a high credit risk. However, the problem in this situation was not whether the banks would collapse and depositors lose their money, but whether the banks would have to be taken into state ownership. Several banks had to be rescued by the state.

In August 1994 the Venezuelan government announced a financial assistance package to rescue two big commercial banks, the Banco de Venezuela, at the time the second largest in the country, and Banco Progreso. A total of eight commercial banks have received government assistance since the Venezuelan banking crisis began in January 1994.

In November 1997 the Japanese banking sector was thrown into turmoil. First Sanyo Securities, the country's seventh largest broker, filed for bankruptcy, the first brokerage to fail since 1945. Then Hokkaido Takushoku, Japan's tenth largest bank collapsed, the first bank to fail since 1945. A week later Yamaichi, the country's fourth largest broker closed the day after Moody's downgraded it to junk-bond status. Finally, at the end of the month Tokuyo City Bank, a small bank, collapsed.

Bank failures are fairly rare although, if nothing else, the Barings case should warn against complacency. A more dangerous credit risk for a borrower is when a bank, perhaps because it is making losses and suffering from a deteriorating balance sheet, or is taking a more aggressive approach to the management of its loan portfolio, decides to reduce the size of the facilities it will grant to a customer.

However, in recent years there have been several reported examples of banks pulling the plug in this way on struggling companies they no longer considered worth supporting. Looking back on some such failures, it is reasonable to ask whether some of these companies collapsed because of their bank. Would another bank have acted differently, and continued to provide support?

Even if a company has a good relationship with its local branch manager or the liaison officer at the bank's regional office, the situation can change dramatically if a new manager is appointed. A new manager normally will begin by reviewing the facilities to existing customers, without the benefit of personal knowledge of the business and its owners and management.

A further risk for companies is that banks in financial difficulties could charge higher margins on their lending, or higher transaction fees. Companies therefore could be made to pay for the problems of the bank. The interest rates offered by banks on loans and on deposits should be compared.

Credit analysis, particularly for bank customer relationships, should be a two-way process. The lender should assess the creditworthiness of its customer, but the borrower should also assess the credit risk in borrowing from any particular bank.

Capital Adequacy

Capital adequacy refers to the need for a bank to have a sizeable base of capital (funds) to protect it from the risk of insolvency.

A high level of company insolvencies exposes commercial banks because bad debts on their loans to failed companies must be financed out of the bank's capital; otherwise the deposits of customers will be at risk. In other words, losses from bad debts on loans reduce the bank's capital funds.

Traditionally banks have tried to protect themselves from the consequences of business failures among customers, and the resulting bad debts, by securing loans against the customer's assets, typically property. A slump in the property markets, however, will erode the value of the collateral security backing many mortgages and business loans. The financial problems of many banks over recent years had their origins in the collapse in property values that began in the late 1980s.

Capital adequacy has become a matter of some concern and banks need to constrain their total lending, in particular their risky lending, to what they can safely afford.

Two broad ways in which capital adequacy can be measured and controlled are by a minimum-leverage ratio or by a minimum-risk asset ratio.

It is useful to look at these concepts, because they provide a basis for banking regulation.

Minimum Leverage Ratio

A bank's balance sheet consists, on the liabilities side, of its own capital and other liabilities, principally deposits of customers.

	$
Capital base (share capital, reserves, other long-term funds)	X
Deposits and other non-capital liabilities	Y
Total liabilities	X+Y

Customer deposits make up by far the largest proportion of liabilities for commercial banks, and far exceed the amount of the banks' own capital.

A leverage ratio approach to measuring and controlling capital adequacy is based on the view that the bank's own capital should be not less than a certain proportion of total liabilities. In other words, a bank should have a minimum leverage ratio. For example, if a minimum leverage ratio is 10%, the ratio of the bank's capital to customer deposits should be not less than 1:9. Deposits should not exceed the value of the bank's capital funds by more than nine times.

Minimum-Risk Asset Ratio

A bank's assets consist mainly of loans and investments. A minimum-risk asset-ratio approach to capital adequacy is based on the view that some assets of a bank are much more risky than others, and that risk should be tightly controlled.

The capital structure of a bank must be sufficiently safe to stand the risk of any losses on its assets, such as bad debts or falling investment values.

These risks consist of

- *Credit risk*, i.e. the possibility that debts owed to the bank will not

be repaid on the due date at their full value
- *Investment risk*, i.e. the risk that investments or other claims held as assets by the bank will fall below their book value (original purchase price)
- *Forced sale risk*, i.e. the risk that when a bank tries to sell the asset, the market is so narrow that it is forced to sell the asset below its book value in a forced sale.

Different types of asset held by banks will carry these risks to a varying extent. Risk assets can be evaluated by multiplying the amount of each asset by a suitable risk weighting of between 0% and 100%. A risky loan would have a 100% risk weighting, whereas cash (till money) would have zero risk. Thus a loan to the US government could be regarded as having nil risk, whereas a loan to a company could have a 100% risk weighting.

Example
Foxtrot Bank has made loans to the government of $60 million, mortgage loans (secured loans) $40 million, and other loans to companies and individuals of $200 million. Risk weightings are nil for loans to the government, 50% for mortgage loans and 100% for other loans.

The bank also has $10 million of investments in government securities that have a 20% risk weighting.

Analysis
The risk-weighted assets of the bank are as follows.

Item	Amount	Risk weighting	Risk-weighted assets
	$m	%	$m
Government loans	60	0	0
Mortgage loans	40	50	20
Other loans	200	100	200
Investments	10	20	2
Total	310		222

Capital adequacy can be measured by a risk-asset ratio. This is a ratio of capital to risk assets. A bank could be required to have a minimum amount of capital as a ratio of the value of its risk-weighted assets. To establish capital adequacy requirements using a risk-asset ratio approach, there must be precise definitions of what constitutes capital, and specifications for how much capital and what type of capital a bank should possess.

Capital adequacy requirements exist in all countries, but vary from one country to another. In view of the complexity of many financial instruments, the regulations themselves can be quite complex.

The Need for Rules on Capital Adequacy

It is now well recognized that there could be a credit risk for any company that deals with a bank. As a consequence of its activities, a bank's capital base could become too low for the volume of customer deposits that it has, and its risk-weighted assets could become too high for its capital base. The risk to customers will be greater when banks compete for market share, and could indulge in indiscriminate lending.

This risk needs to be controlled, to preserve confidence in the banking system, and a bank should have enough capital to support the volume and nature of its business transactions. It has been recognized that since banking is a competitive and international business, there should be compulsory regulation over capital adequacy rather than voluntary controls, and the regulations should be based on international agreement.

The Basle Agreement

An international agreement between central banking authorities, known as the Basle Agreement, was reached in December 1987. The central banks are members of the Bank for International Settlements (BIS), and the agreement is also referred to as the BIS Agreement. Its aims are to apply a common set of rules for capital adequacy to all banks in international banking, and thereby prevent some banks having unfair advantages over others. The objectives are to reduce the risks of an international bank failing. Each country subscribing to the agreement has introduced regulations for its domestic banking system that are based on those rules.

The agreement contains both a minimum-risk asset-ratio requirement and a minimum leverage requirement. For the minimum-risk, asset-ratio requirement, it defines a bank's capital, and sets out rules for deciding how much capital a bank should have to support its risk-weighted assets. This applies to off-balance-sheet assets as well as straight lending. It also applies to a bank's offshore activities as well as to its domestic operations and assets.

The agreement sets certain targets or requirements for capital adequacy that all international banks must achieve. These targets are as follows

- a minimum capital:risk-assets ratio of 8%. In other words, a bank's capital must be at least 8% of the risk-weighted value of its assets. Risk assets are measured by multiplying the value of each class of assets by a stated risk factor applicable to that class. The scale of risk runs from zero to 100%
- a minimum core equity:total capital base ratio of 50%. A bank must have at least 50% of its capital as core equity. A bank's capital base consists of Tier 1 and Tier 2 capital. Tier 1 capital is core equity, but Tier 2 is not
- a minimum core equity:total assets ratio of 4%. This is a form of minimum leverage requirement.

Tier 1 and Tier 2 Capital

Qualifying capital is divided into two levels or tiers.

- Tier 1 consists of fully paid up ordinary stock capital, non-cumulative perpetual preference stock and disclosed reserves (retained profits, share premium account etc.).
- Tier 2 consists of supplementary capital, and includes revaluation

reserves, unrealized capital gains on securities owned by the bank, hidden reserves and general provisions. It also includes hybrid debt instruments and subordinated term debt.

At least 50% of a bank's capital must be Tier 1 capital. Subordinated debt will qualify as Tier 2 capital only up to 50% of the amount of Tier 1 capital.

Risk-Adjusted Weightings to Assets

A bank's assets are given a risk-weighted valuation. The risk weighting given to a particular type of asset is an assessment of its credit risk for the bank. Risk weightings are given to off-balance-sheet assets as well as to on-balance-sheet assets. Risk asset values are therefore given to NIFs, RUFs, documentary credits and other contingent liabilities or guarantees, swaps and futures.

General guidelines for risk weightings divide on-balance-sheet assets into four broad groups.

Group	Risk weighting
Claims on the domestic government	Nil
Short-term claims on other banks	20%
Mortgage loans to owner-occupiers	50%
Other claims on the private sector	100%

Private sector loans for first mortgages secured on a residential property have a 50% risk weight.

Risk weights are given to assets for which there are no credit risks, but for which there is an investment risk. These are assets that might lose value because of an adverse change in interest rates; for example investments in gilts are given some risk weighting because they would fall in price if market interest rates were to rise.

Example
The assets of Omega Bank are listed in the table overleaf. Risk asset values for these assets are also shown.

MEASURING CREDIT RISK

	Assets	Risk weights	Risk assets
	$m	%	$m
Notes, coin, deposits with the Federal Reserve	200	0	0
Treasury bills	100	0	0
Eligible bank bills	500	20	100
Money market loans	2,600	20	520
Long-term loans			
Central	100	0	0
Government	1,000	50	500
Private sector: first mortgages	10,000	100	10,000
Investments in US Securities (all over one year)	200	20	40
	14,700		11,160

Analysis

Risk asset values also will be calculated for off-balance-sheet assets, and added to the bank's total risk assets.

Under the Basle rules, that were in the process of being fully revised in 1999, if we assume that Omega Bank has no off-balance-sheet assets, the bank must have capital funds of at least $892.8 million, 8% of its risk-weighted assets (8% of $11,160 million). Of this minimum funding, at least 50% or $446.4 million must consist of Tier 1 capital.

However, the bank's Tier 1 capital must be at least 4% of its total assets, i.e. at least $568 million (4% of $14,700 million).

If the bank had $570 million of Tier 1 capital and $330 million of Tier 2 capital, giving a total capital base of $900 million, it would be just within the present Basle rules for capital adequacy. It would need to avoid loss-making activities, such as making bad loans, because losses would reduce its capital base below $900 million, and, if the losses were large enough, force it to reduce its risk-weighted assets and also to seek extra Tier 1 funds.

Amendments to the Basle Agreement

For banks with substantial investment banking operations, the BIS has acknowledged that traditional asset risk weightings are not necessarily appropriate and has agreed that banks should be allowed to use their own internal models to calculate how much capital they require.

Amendments to the BIS rules to take better care of market risks became effective in 1998 although the US Federal Reserve allowed some banks to adopt the rules sooner because banking supervisors were satisfied that their models worked properly. The first institution to take advantage of this change was Bankers Trust that received approval in early 1997.

The European Commission that agreed similar changes under its 1996 Capital Adequacy Directive (Cad II) also covers European banks.

Under the new system a bank measures its value at risk, i.e. the amount it would be expected to lose in 99 trading periods out of 100, a trading period being ten days. The number is then multiplied by three to give the required capital cushion. Usually this will still leave banks needing to hold less capital than under the old rules, but banks still believe that the new rules require them to hold too much capital.

Implications of the Basle Agreement

Each country is allowed to apply its own capital adequacy rules using the Basle Agreement as a basic minimum. The possible consequences of this agreement are significant. If the major banks in all the industrialized countries conform to the same regulations about capital adequacy, competitive inequalities should be removed. A bank in country X won't be able to win more international business just because it is allowed to operate with a lower capital base:risk-asset ratio than banks in other countries, i.e. it can carry out more lending than other countries' banking authorities would regard as safe.

Capital adequacy regulations for banks also have several implications for companies.

- *Reduction in credit risk.* Banks should be less likely to collapse and go into liquidation.
- *Refusal to lend or to offer services.* The volume of business that a bank can handle is restricted by the minimum capital adequacy ratio. If a bank's capital base is close to its minimum-risk asset ratio, it might refuse to grant extra facilities to a customer, or to sell extra services to which risk weightings would be attached.
- *Withdrawal of lending facilities.* The most serious problems occur when a bank's capital base is nearing its minimum-risk asset ratio and is still making losses, so that its capital base is contracting. In these circumstances, a bank could be forced to cut back its total lending; for example by refusing to renew customers' borrowing facilities. A bank could suddenly reduce a customer's overdraft facility, through no fault of the customer.
- *Higher charges.* Banks are likely to make higher charges for services with a high risk weighting.

For a bank that is close to its minimum ratio, its ability to increase the volume of its business will be restricted by the need to increase its capital, with Tier 1 capital having to be at least 50% of total capital. Increases in Tier 1 capital must come mainly from retained profits, and so banks must operate at a profit, or be able to raise new issues of share capital. If its Tier 1 capital is over 50% of its total capital, new issues of subordinated debt could be preferred.

When a bank's profits are poor, investors might be reluctant to subscribe for new issues of its shares or subordinated debt. This could create severe difficulties for the bank. In the second half of 1997, for example, investors were unwilling to subscribe for South Korean bank paper except at very high yields because of the banking crisis in that country.

The Basle rules have had a noticeable impact on bank lending, affecting both pricing and the availability of loans. Because of capital adequacy regulations, companies should be even more careful than in the past about choosing the bank or banks with which to deal.

Credit Analysis on Banks

A company wishing to borrow extensively or to place large deposits with a bank should check its capital adequacy ratios. It should be able to estimate from a bank's published accounts

- an equity capital/total assets ratio
- a Tier 1 capital/total assets ratio.

Example
When US Swiss banks SBC and UBS announced their planned merger in 1997 to become the United Bank of Switzerland, UBS was regarded as the weaker of the two banks, with reported ratios at the time as follows

	SBC	UBS
Common equity/assets		
Tier 1 capital/assets		

These ratios are fairly close to the minimum levels that would be expected. By comparing banks, it is possible to build up a picture of which banks are in a better position to expand their loan book than others are – and be a smaller credit risk to the borrower or depositor.

Liquidity
A company can do further credit analysis by looking at the bank's financial statements in its annual report and accounts. In addition to capital adequacy, it can check the bank's liquidity by measuring the proportion of the bank's total assets that are liquid.

$$\text{Liquid assets ratio} = \frac{\text{Liquid assets}}{\text{Total assets}} \times 100\%$$

Liquid assets consist of cash, balances with the central bank, money market loans and short-term investments. The liquidity ratios of banks can be compared.

When liquidity is low and declining from one year to the next, the poor liquidity could act as a constraint on further lending by the bank, because this would reduce its liquidity still further.

Other Factors

The economic strength of the bank's host country can be relevant to a company that is considering borrowing from an international bank. It should be wary of borrowing too heavily from a bank in a less-developed country, or even from a bank in a country where the banking system generally appears to be in financial difficulty.

In the event of the bank getting into financial difficulties, companies shouldn't rely on the government or the rest of the banking system to bail it out, and taking on its loan book. Much of this is subjective judgment, and borrowing decisions by a company shouldn't be based on this consideration alone.

Using Bank Risk Information

Assessing banks can influence a company's decision about which bank or banks to approach for loans or other credit-related transactions. A bank's own financial position can affect its response to customer approaches, including the interest rate it would like to charge on lending.

Cash-rich companies also can use bank risk information to choose a bank for placing cash on deposit. In setting limits it is important to ensure that the total limit with each bank or group of banks is well in excess of the company's maximum expected cash surplus.

Example
Delta expects to have a maximum cash surplus of $50 million in the next 12 months. It deposits money with four banks, East Bank, North Bank, South Bank and Foxtrot Bank. East, North and South Banks all have a double-A credit rating. Foxtrot Bank has a single-A credit rating. Delta's board of directors wants to impose limits on the deposits that its treasurer can place with each bank.

Analysis

The total of the limits for the four banks should be well in excess of $50 million, to give the treasurer room for maneuver. If the limits totaled just $50 million, the treasurer would have no choice about where to deposit the company's cash when it reached its peak, and Delta would then have to accept whatever interest rate each bank cared to offer.

The board of directors also could decide to set a higher limit for banks with a higher credit rating.

The credit limits could be selected as follows

Bank	Credit rating	Maximum limit
		$m
East	AA	25
North	AA	25
South	AA	25
Centre	A	15
Total		90

Guidelines

Knowledge of the possible consequences of the Basle Agreement can only warn companies about the credit risk of relying on bank borrowing, but it cannot help the company to select the bank or banks with which it should carry out its business.

Depositing Money

Companies should use surplus cash to earn interest. For fairly small amounts of cash, it is sensible to find out what rates the company's bank will offer. Shopping round for better rates isn't worth the effort when the amount involved is small.

Large amounts of cash are a different proposition, and credit risk becomes a factor. When the Bank of Credit and Commerce International was closed down in 1991, it emerged that the local authority for the

Western Isles of Scotland had deposited over £20 million with the bank. Other authorities had deposited amounts, often using a money-broking firm to place the deposits, not making any credit checks on the banks where funds were deposited. The attraction of BCCI was apparently the high interest rate that it paid to depositors, an extra $1/_2$% on £20 million is worth £100,000 extra income every year.

As the British Prime Minister John Major commented at the time, the credit risk problem is that higher returns are earned only by taking a higher risk.

For large deposits, the risk should be spread. If a company wants to earn more interest, it can place deposits with some smaller, perhaps riskier banks, but it would be unwise to put all its eggs in one basket. Deposits should be spread among different banks, and if one collapses, the loss should not provoke a cash flow crisis in the company.

Borrowing Money
Deciding where to borrow, and how much, is a different problem. Small companies could have little choice. Normally they will have a relationship with just one clearing bank that could arrange an overdraft facility or a loan. A company can change banks, but not often or regularly. If a company is in debt to its existing bank, switching to another bank is not always easy. The bank that is invited to take on the account will look at the company carefully before agreeing.

Larger companies have more choice. Even many medium-sized companies can borrow from more than one bank if they choose. The credit problems then become

- which bank or banks to borrow from, and
- how much of the total borrowings should be sought from each bank.

The risk/return balance to be considered by a company is that the banks offering the lower interest rates are the ones that are most likely to pull the plug if the company runs into difficulties. And if more banks are involved in lending, it is more likely that one of them will become difficult at some stage. A wide geographical spread of lending banks can also cause difficulties.

Bank Relationships and Monitoring Banks
It is vital that a company gets to know its bankers. It is easier to deal with a familiar individual than an impersonal voice at the end of a telephone. If a company were reluctant to borrow because it is concerned that the bank could withdraw its facilities at some time, a more open relationship with the bank would enable the company to discuss its concern.

A company should be informed about the current activities and policies of its banks. Newspaper and journal reports are a useful source of information. The press is very sensitive to the behavior of banks. If any bank develops a reputation for withdrawing customer support, it could be reported in the financial press.

It can be helpful to look for the amount of write-downs or bad debt write-offs that the bank has made. Usually these are discussed in the press whenever a bank declares its financial results. When a bank is making large bad debts its management will be seeking to stem the tide of future losses. This will have implications for its lending decisions and interest rates on its loans.

It might be possible to obtain information about the nature of the bank's lending book. A high-risk lending book might consist of large exposures to emerging market economies or to regions or sectors experiencing a severe economic downturn, such as the crisis in Asia. At the start of a recession, it might be to property and construction companies.

Setting and Policing Credit Limits

Previous chapters have discussed the various methods and sources of external and inhouse credit assessments. Such assessments are useful only when they lead to a decision about granting or refusing credit, deciding the credit terms to offer and setting credit limits.

Credit assessments and decisions about granting credit should be part of an established system in the credit management process. Such systems ensure that the right questions are asked and suitable assurances are obtained. Also they should ensure that all customers are treated fairly, although distinctions normally will be made between large and small customers, and between new and existing clients.

There must be a clear division of responsibilities between senior management at head office and local operational management. Credit policy normally will be set at head office, providing guidelines or limits to the total credit that should be allowed.

Day-to-day credit decisions should be set by operations management within a set of guidelines. These guidelines could be produced at operations level for each division of the business region. Alternatively, they can be set by head office.

Decisions involving large amounts of credit could be referred from divisional or operational level to head office. This decision-making structure is typical of retail banks, where lending decisions are centralized in a head office limit, and smaller lending decisions are delegated to local managers operating within head office guidelines.

Setting Credit Limits: Total Credit

Individual credit decisions should be made within the framework of a total credit limit for individual divisions and for the company as a whole. This limit should be consistent with the organization's credit strategy.

At a policy-making level, there are several factors that should influence credit-setting decisions including

- the overall scale of the bad debt risk. In a recession, when the risk is high, credit limits should be reduced
- the total credit limit (or risk) that the company can afford. A balance has to be reached between the potential returns from extra credit sales, or loans, in the case of banks and the cost of bad debts and interest on the capital invested in the extra debtors
- the existing volume of debtors. Policy decisions cannot ignore existing conditions
- country risk and industry risk, and the desirability of setting country limits or industry limits for credit
- the target average period of credit that should be allowed.

A target credit period could be set, perhaps with reference to the current norm in the industry. For example, if a company expects annual sales turnover of $12 million, with all sales on credit, and the industry norm is to offer one month's credit, the company could set a total credit limit in the region of $1 million ($1/_{12} \times$ $12 million).

The maximum permissible amount of trade debtors could be expressed either as a specific amount of money or as a percentage of sales. The appropriate ceiling will vary according to the nature of the business and what credit has been permitted in the past.

The total credit limit for a company could be set at perhaps no more than 80% of sales in the previous two months. This policy would then set a credit limit based on average debtor days of 1.6 months (2 months × 80%). Debtor days is an approximate measure of the average period of credit taken by customers. Subsequently the credit limit can be monitored. If it is breached, the credit manager can be asked to explain why and what has been done to bring total credit back within the limit.

Example

Alpha is a company with three operating divisions. Credit decisions are taken at divisional level by local management. Alpha's board of directors has decided that total customer credit should not exceed $7 million, and limits for each division have been set as follows

	Credit limit	
Division 1	$3 million	
Division 2	$2.5 million	
Division 3	$2.5 million	$8 million
Alpha-total	$7 million	

The credit limit for the three individual divisions taken in total, is $8 million. This exceeds the limit for Alpha as a whole by $1 million. This is not an error of arithmetic.

Alpha's directors presumably consider that because of the seasonal nature of their businesses, the individual divisional limits totalling $8 million and the total company limit of $7 million are not inconsistent.

However, divisional management should report when total debtors are approaching or exceed the limit, and indicate the action being taken to keep credit under control.

Why is a Total Credit Limit Necessary?

A limit on total credit allowed should be set for several reasons. Debtors have to be financed. Debtors represent sales not yet paid for, but for which the company has incurred various expenditures. They can be financed in one of two ways

- by taking short-term credit, chiefly from suppliers or as a bank overdraft, or
- by increasing long-term funds.

If an increase in debtors is financed by an increase in short-term creditors, there will be implications for the company's liquidity. This could affect the company's own credit rating with its banks and suppliers.

If an increase in debtors is financed by an increase in long-term funds, there could be an inefficient use of capital. It could affect the company's return on capital and earnings per share.

In setting a limit for total credit, the debtor days principle can be applied. Debtor days represent the period on average for which sales remain unpaid. The term average sales outstanding is also often used. This principle states that the average credit period taken by customers should not exceed a certain length. For example, if a total credit limit is 15% of turnover, this means that average debtor days should not exceed about 55 days (15% × 365). Setting such a limit imposes strict discipline on debtor management.

Granting credit has a cost that ought to be recognized when monitoring profitability or setting sales prices. For example, if a company regularly allows customers to take two months' credit and interest costs are 12%, the cost of credit would add 2% ($^{2}/_{12}$ × 12%) to the cost of sales, and would reduce net profits accordingly. This size cost can be significant.

Credit Limits for Individual Countries
Within the overall credit limit, limits also can be set for individual countries. This is particularly relevant for international companies that sell regularly into developing or less-developed countries, and for international banks. Country limits and industry limits were discussed in Chapter 6.

Setting Credit Limits for Individual Companies

An individual credit limit must be set for new customers and kept under regular review for existing customers. Factors to consider are

- typical order sizes and the price of the goods or services
- typical frequency of ordering
- standard settlement terms for the industry
- credit rating or assessment of the customer
- the customer's payment record, in the case of existing customers.

In many companies, credit managers will be allowed to use their discretion in individual cases, subject to overall policy guidelines. However, there are two basic systems that can be used.

Standing Starting Credit Limits

A company can establish a standard credit limit for new customers, based on a typical order size and normal settlement terms. Each new customer will be granted credit up to this limit, subject to a satisfactory credit assessment. For example, a company might allow new customers credit up to $3,000 on terms of 30 days net from the invoice date.

The credit limit for each customer can be adjusted over time according to

- its anticipated volume of demand
- any price increases for the company's goods or services
- a satisfactory payment record by the customer, and
- a continuing satisfactory credit assessment.

Of course any of these these adjustments to credit limits should be negotiated with the customer.

Inhouse Credit Ratings

A company's credit management team can establish its own credit ratings for customers, based perhaps on the rating system of a credit information agency or, in some industries, a credit rating agency. There could be a scale of ratings, for example from one to five, with a rating of one indicating a top-quality, low-credit-risk customer and a rating of five indicating an unknown customer or a high credit risk. Also credit limits can be set for each bank. Within this type of system, the credit manager should be prepared to upgrade an existing customer's rating when his credit rating improves, and also to downgrade the rating if his credit risk increases.

Within any system of credit setting, there should be scope for exceptional cases, but these can be referred to a senior manager for an assessment and credit decision. Individual managers should accept responsibility for any exceptional decision.

Example
Beta is approached by a new customer asking to purchase goods worth $3,000 on credit. The customer has indicated that he will probably place this size order five or six times a year, and would like credit terms of 30 days net after the invoice date.

Beta's credit manager has obtained an assessment of the customer from a rating agency that indicates the customer has a record of paying invoices about 30 days after the due date.

Analysis
Beta's credit manager must use his or her judgment with this new customer. The customer has indicated that its credit requirement should never exceed about $3,000. However, in view of the customer's credit assessment, it seems quite possible that the customer could at some time require credit for two deliveries of goods. The credit manager nevertheless could fix a credit limit at about $3,000-$4,000, and monitor the customer's payments over time. Alternatively, if the customer is regarded as a low credit risk, a credit limit of about $6,000-$7,000, sufficient for two orders could be allowed from the outset.

There are likely to be standard industry credit terms that customers will expect to receive, such as

- net 30 days from date of invoice
- net 30 days from date of delivery
- end of the month following the month of invoice.

Some customers organize check runs on specific days each month, such as the 21st of each month, or the nearest working day to the 21st. In these cases, a credit manager could extend trade credit on terms such as the next check run date, perhaps the 21st of the month, following 30 days after invoice date.

Settlement discounts can be offered for earlier payment, but this is more a matter for cash flow management than credit management. However, if a customer regularly takes early settlement discounts, this would be a sign of strong cash flow or good liquidity, and the customer's credit rating could be upgraded accordingly.

The credit limits of individual customers should be reviewed regularly, ideally before a customer asks for his limit to be increased. It helps to have an answer ready to a customer's request for more credit because a delayed response to any such request, either favorable or unfavorable, could damage the relationship with the customer. If the request is refused, the customer has the immediate opportunity to protest, and ask for a reconsidered opinion.

Monitoring Credit

Credit must be monitored continually.

- Overdue payments must be chased. This is routine credit management.
- The payment record of individual customers should be used to reassess their credit rating and credit limit.
- At some stage, a decision might have to be taken about writing off a debt as uncollectable, or pursuing the customer through the judicial system. A company's bad debts record should be a factor in the regular reassessment of credit policy.

Monitoring reports on customer credit vary from company to company and bank to bank. The most commonly used report for monitoring individual customers is the aged debtors' report. This is simply a list of customers who owe money, the total owed and the period of time for which money has been owed.

The format of reports can vary widely. Some reports show the credit terms and list the amounts owed according to whether they are overdue and if so, how long they have been overdue. Other reports simply list unpaid amounts by showing the length of time since the invoice date.

The report can have a comments column, to record any action taken to obtain an overdue payment.

If an individual customer has exceeded his credit limit, the credit manager should be expected to sort out the problem and to explain to senior management how or why the limit was breached in the first place.

A special report can be prepared on the customers whose accounts have been overdue for the longest time, as shown below.

Aged Debtors' Report
Gamma Limited

Data as at: 30/04/1999   Report produced on May 6 1999

Code	Customer	Total	Current	1 Month	2 Months	3 Months	4 Months	Comments
465	Able	3,955.93	0.00	3,955.93	0.00	0.00	0.00	
733	Baker	13,484.45	376.45	2,020.57	0.00	11,087.43	0.00	*
216	Delta	13,130.27	13,130.27	0.00	0.00	0.00	0.00	
156	Echo	11,004.63	1,004.63	8,000.00	2,000.00	0.00	0.00	
231	Foxtrot	5,914.37	2,914.37	0.00	3,000.00	0.00	0.00	
204	Indigo	2,408.75	2,408.75	0.00	0.00	0.00	0.00	
254	Tango	5,041.00	0.00	0.00	0.00	0.00	5,041.00	*
113	Victor	2,347.45	1,587.45	760.00	0.00	0.00	0.00	
Total outstanding		57,286.85	21,421.92	14,736.50	5,000.00	11,087.43	5,041.00	

*1   Customer chased April 29. Payment promised by May 5.

*2   Judicial proceedings were being prepared.

Aged Debtors' Exception Report

The five largest overdue accounts, overdue by more than 30 days

	Name	Last 12 months' sales	Total due	Amounts Overdue 31/60 days	61/90 days	90/120 days	120+ days	Credit limit
1.	Saturn	$60,000	$35,000	$8,000	$12,000	$9,000	$6,000	$30,000
2.	Mercury	$8,000	$6,000		$6,000			$6,000
3.	Neptune	$12,000	$6,000	$3,000		$3,000		$7,000
4.	Orion	$5,000	$5,000				$5,000	$5,000
5.	Pluto	$25,000	$15,000		$5,000		$10,000	$16,000

Comments: Why Overdue? Action Taken: Basis For Extending Credit

1. Saturn — Regular customer. Credit for $8,000 given over one month ago after discussions with customer. Customer being pressed for payments of $15,000.
2. Mercury — Customer at credit limit. Credit rating being reassessed. Payment expected within seven days.
3. Neptune — Payment of $3,000 expected shortly.
4. Orion — Court action being taken.
5. Pluto — Customer reported serious financial difficulties one month ago. Probable bad debt.

Customers whose accounts are reported as exceptionally late payments probably will have their credit limit reassessed. The customer should be notified of any such change in advance. When dealing with large customers, the credit manager should discuss the payment problem with the customer before reaching any decision about reducing the credit limit.

Policing Total Credit Limits

Total credit limits, as well as individual credit limits and payment records, should be monitored continually. An aged debtors' list and exception report, as described above, can provide control information to operational credit managers. Senior management also should receive regular reports to show whether there is adherence to their policy for total credit limits.

A credit utilization report can be prepared to show the extent to which customers are using their credit limits.

Credit Utilization Report

Customer	Limit	Utilization	Margin	Comments
	$000	$000	$000	
XYZ	100	6	94	
ABC	50	45	5	
DEF	120	95	25	
NOP	30	32	-2	Authorized by board, 16 March
Total	300	178		
Utilization	59.3%			

SETTING AND POLICING CREDIT LIMITS

A report on credit utilization can be used to identify customers who might soon want further credit. Also it can indicate whether the company's policy on overall credit limits could be acting as a constraint on credit sales. A utilization of 90%, for example, would indicate that many customers are at or near their credit limit, suggesting that the company's credit policy is very tight.

In addition, the bad debt record should be monitored. If bad debts are higher than budgeted, there should be a decision regarding how much to tighten up credit procedures; grant less credit, chase up late payers more vigorously, etc. and whether to accept the higher level of bad debts as a necessary evil in return for the benefits of higher sales and profits.

If there is a record of few bad debts, management could have the confidence to raise the level of credit limits in order to win more sales.

Example
Credit utilization can be analyzed by industry within a country, or by country within an industry.

Trade Debtors' Analysis as at December 31

Industry	Current credit utilization $000	% of total creditors %	Annual sales $million	As a % of sales %
Property	9,480	25.0	140.2	18.4
Construction	7,640	20.2	140.1	18.4
Engineering	4,350	11.5	112.6	14.8
Electricals	4,000	10.6	83.7	11.8
Electricity	2,170	5.7	49.2	6.5
Transport	3,230	8.5	79.9	10.5
Chemicals, plastics	1,860	4.9	43.3	5.7
Motors, aircraft trades	5,170	13.6	105.8	13.9
	37,900	100%	760.6	100%

Analysis
An industry analysis of credit exposure shows in this case that over 45% of the company's trade debtors (about $17 million) are in the property

and construction industries. The company's management ought to have a view about this exposure to industry risk.

The size of the exposure to property and construction could seem excessive, in view of the cyclical nature of these industries, the current economic outlook, and the comparatively slow payment rate from these customers. These industries account for only 36.8% of annual sales, but 45.2% of trade debtors. Management might wish to consider whether the company should try to reduce this exposure.

A decision might be required about whether the company should be willing to accumulate trade debtors in these sectors, in order to sustain sales, or whether the credit risk would be too high.

Summary

Credit limits should be set and monitored within the framework of an established credit management system. A brief checklist for a credit limit policy and monitoring system is as follows

The answer should be yes to the following questions.

- Is there an established system within the organization for trade credit risk assessment, leading to the setting of credit limits?
- Are credit limits being set, in total and for individual customers?
- Are breaches of credit terms and limits reported?
- Are breaches of credit terms and limits acted upon when they occur?
- Are credit limits reviewed and altered regularly, in total and for individual customers?
- Is the level of bad debts experienced by the organization consistent with credit risk policy and sales targets?
- Does the organization have a policy for using credit insurance or non-recourse factoring?
- Does the organization have a policy for encouraging more secure methods of payment, such as payment in advance or confirmed letters of credit?

Policing of credit limits involves continually reviewing customers. Although a customer's payment record can be monitored, this on its own is not sufficient to judge the company's bad debt risks. Methods should be applied for identifying when an existing customer has become a higher credit risk and what to do in the situation. Credit deterioration is the subject of the next chapter.

Credit Deterioration

Credit analysis should be a continuous process. Decisions to grant credit can be reviewed in light of the customer's payment record and any additional information that can be obtained over time. The credit manager should be looking for evidence to warrant an increase in a customer's credit, should this be requested, and for evidence of credit deterioration and greater credit risk.

Cycle of Credit Monitoring and Decisionmaking

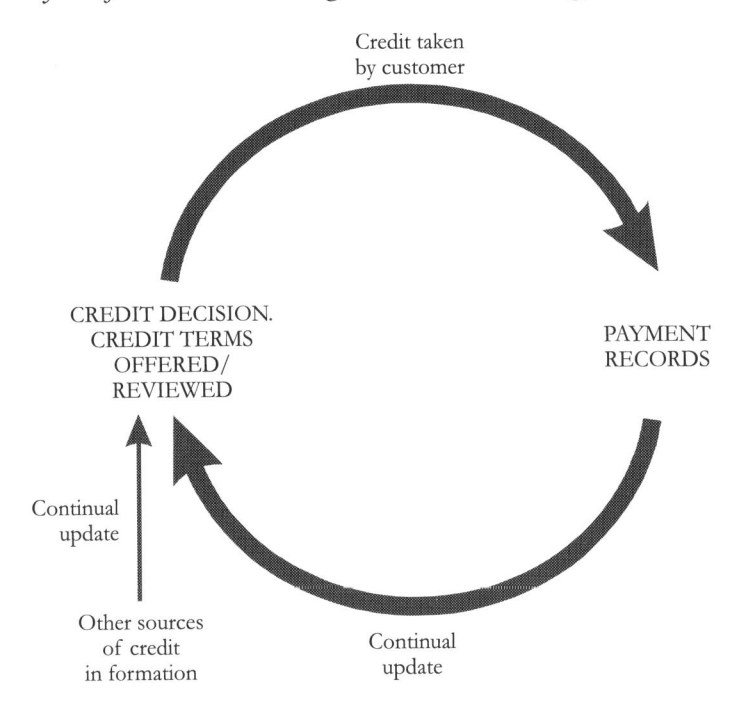

```
                    Credit taken
                    by customer
                         ↓

    CREDIT DECISION.              PAYMENT
    CREDIT TERMS                  RECORDS
    OFFERED/
    REVIEWED
         ↑
    Continual
     update

    Other sources              Continual
      of credit                 update
    in formation
```

Indicators of Credit Deterioration

There are various pointers to a deterioration in the credit risk of customers. Some of these can indicate an immediate and serious credit risk; others could suggest the possibility of greater credit risk at some future time. These indicators of deterioration have already been described in this book.

- The customer's payment record.
- Financial ratio analysis, carried out on each new set of accounts produced by the customer.
- Update on the customer, e.g. a new status report, from a credit information agency.
- Downrating by a credit rating agency.
- Being placed on credit watch with negative implications by a credit rating agency.
- A new credit rating based on a credit scoring system or a Z score model. Z scores are described in *Corporate Credit Analysis*, another title in this series.
- New information made public about the company, such as press comments or a court action for debt collection involving the customer.
- A run on the company's share price.
- A delayed announcement of the company's annual results.
- Reports that the company is paying abnormally high interest on its funds.
- Insolvency: receivership or administration.

Payment Record

A customer's payment record is one of the most reliable indicators of credit deterioration. The credit controller can look for information in the customer's credit history of

- late payments and difficulties in obtaining payment, checks lost in the post or checks that have to be collected by courier from the customer, etc.

- round sum payments, e.g. payment of $5,000 on account when $10,749 is owed
- disputes about invoices for minor reasons
- incorrectly prepared checks
- unsigned checks.

A troublesome payer is often hiding cash flow difficulties.

Unfortunately for the supplier, governments cannot force customers to pay on time, and mere words of encouragement are of little practical value. Getting customers to pay on time depends on the commercial relationship between the supplier or bank, and the customer, the customer's attitude, and the efficiency of credit control within the supplier organization or the bank.

Another warning sign could be when the customer stops taking an early settlement discount and starts taking the full period of credit allowed. If the discount is financially attractive, and a customer stops taking it, there would be a suspicion that the customer is starting to have cash flow problems, and needs to take the longer credit.

Financial Ratio Analysis

Financial ratio analysis can provide pointers to credit deterioration. Any worsening trend in the financial ratios of a company can be a cause for concern and prompt a downgrading of the customer's credit rating.

Checks should be kept in particular on

- decreasing profitability
- decreasing sales turnover
- changes in the amount of cash held by the company between one balance sheet date and the next
- any increase in total debt, as well as higher financial leverage
- a restricted or unusual dividend policy such as the offer of shares instead of cash as a dividend or dividends higher than the current year's profits.

Other Pointers to Credit Deterioration

Press reports about companies in financial difficulties often emerge at quite a late stage in the credit deterioration process because, correctly, the press must respect libel laws. The press should not be the catalyst for making a company's financial troubles even worse by publishing reports about the company.

However, press reports can give useful warning. Information about court actions for the non-payment of debts, another indication of potential credit risk, can be obtained from specialist publications or a credit reference agency.

A run on the share price of a public company is an indication of lack of shareholder confidence. If the share price of a company falls sharply, the reason will be the expectation that profits and dividends will be much less than previously anticipated. This is not to suggest that the company is in danger of insolvency. However, companies whose shares are at their low point for the year are also potentially high credit risks and any subsequent movement in the share price should be monitored closely.

When a large company obtains new loans, and the cost of the loans is reported, the rate of interest payable could indicate the financial health of the borrower. Paying over the odds for a loan indicates a high credit risk assessment on the borrower by the lending bank.

Downgrading of large companies, or banks, by a credit rating agency is also a useful pointer to credit risk, especially for organizations that grant large amounts of credit to those companies, or deposit large amounts of cash with it.

Chapter 11

A company that is in financial difficulties can go into liquidation under Chapter 7 of the Bankruptcy Code. Alternatively, it can file for protection under Chapter 11 of the Code. Companies that have filed for Chapter 11 protection should be regarded as high credit risks.

Chapter 11 is an approach to reorganizing a company that is facing bankruptcy, and it differs from the practice of appointing a receiver as used in the UK, Australia and Canada. It is similar in some respects, however, to an administration order.

A company that has filed for protection under Chapter 11 is allowed to continue in business under its own management but subject to certain rules and procedures. It is given protection from its creditors who were still unpaid at the time that it petitioned for Chapter 11 protection. There is an intention, not always successfully achieved, of emerging from Chapter 11 at some future time.

Some major companies that have filed for Chapter 11 protection in recent years have been Texaco, TWA and US Lines, the container shipping company.

It can be important for credit managers to understand the implications of dealing with a company that is in Chapter 11 or that has just filed for Chapter 11. For example, if a customer has just filed for Chapter 11, what does this imply for an existing debt, or for a delivery of goods about to be made?

Outline of Chapter 11 Rules

A company that is in debt files a voluntary petition with the court for protection under Chapter 11. The company does not have to be insolvent to do this. When one company in a group files, there is no obligation for all companies in the group to file. Subsidiaries incorporated abroad are specifically not allowed to file.

If it is a listed company, its shares will continue to be quoted and traded on the stock exchange but with a symbol identifying it clearly as a Chapter 11 company.

When the petition is filed, there is an automatic stay of actions by all existing creditors. The amounts owed to these creditors are called pre-petition liabilities that are categorized into secured and unsecured liabilities. Secured liabilities eventually will be paid in full or up to the realized value of the secured assets. Unsecured liabilities are unlikely ever to be paid in full.

The company is therefore relieved from the pressures of having to pay its old creditors but must be able to pay any new creditors from its continuing trading operations.

A committee of unsecured creditors is established with a separate committee in some cases for secured creditors. This acts as a watchdog over the company's management that continues to run the business. However, the management must obtain advance authorization from the bankruptcy court for certain transactions, such as new borrowings, a significant asset sale, selling stock at a large discount or entering into executory contracts. Executory contracts include contracts of employment, long-term leases and construction contracts. At the time of filing under Chapter 11, the company can reject executory contracts and if the other contractee claims damages, this claim would be an unsecured pre-petition liability.

Chapter 11 protection can last for a long time, typically between two and eight years. Eventually, the company could emerge from Chapter 11 protection, having reached an agreement with its pre-petition creditors. Unsecured creditors might have to accept a mixture of cash, debt securities and equity as payment. For example, steel producer Wheeling-Pittsburgh was under Chapter 11 protection between 1985 and 1991, and on emerging paid its unsecured creditors ¢71 in the dollar.

The main characteristics of a Chapter 11 reorganization are summarized in the table overleaf.

> The Main Characteristics of a Chapter 11 Reorganization
>
> 1. Accepting the petition protects the company from its pre-petition creditors. Unsecured pre-petition creditors will not be paid until the company emerges from Chapter 11 protection.
>
> 2. The company continues to trade, often under its existing management (although sometimes managed by a trustee).
>
> 3. The company's management tries to formulate a reorganization plan.
>
> 4. Once a plan is adopted by the court, the company's debt payments are limited by an agreed schedule and the amounts specified in this plan. The court is unlikely to approve the plan unless the pre-petition creditors and the shareholders agree to accept it.
>
> 5. Proceedings can be complex and last several years.
>
> 6. When the company finally emerges from Chapter 11 proceedings, it will be a restructured company, normally under different control. For example, pre-petition unsecured creditors usually will take equity as part-payment.

If the company doesn't emerge from Chapter 11, creditors could receive less than if the company had gone into immediate liquidation instead of trying a Chapter 11 rescue plan. This could have happened in the case of Eastern Airlines in 1990, when the judge refused an application by creditors to put the company into immediate liquidation.

Credit Management and Chapter 11 Customers

When a company trades with a company that has filed for Chapter 11 protection it must take certain measures. A provision will have to be made for losses on the unpaid pre-petition debts, since these debts cannot be chased and payment is now uncertain. If the amount owed is substantial, the company might want representation on the committee of unsecured creditors.

A company obviously will be wary of continuing to trade with a company operating under Chapter 11 protection and possible options are

- to refuse to trade
- to place strict limits on the amount of credit allowed
- to impose strict payment terms
- to insist on cash on delivery or cash before delivery.

Summary

When a customer shows signs of credit deterioration the information should be fed into the decisionmaking process for credit management. Where companies have a credit-scoring system, the customer's rating will be downgraded, and credit limits revised.

Monitoring credit risk is simply part of the continuing credit assessment process, and the amount of resources that any company commits to this activity should depend on bad-debt experience and the potential costs and consequences of the credit risks involved.

The toughest decisions on credit deterioration often will be taken by banks and because banks are often the prime movers in such events, their procedures for monitoring credit deterioration are particularly important.

Conclusion

Credit risk is unavoidable, but it should be kept within tolerable limits. To achieve control over the risk, a system of measurement and monitoring is needed. The purpose of this book has been to look at the sources and use of information for credit control.

A Control System for Risk

A system to control credit risk should have four elements

- a policy for credit
- vetting individual customers
- efficient operational procedures
- monitoring the performance of credit management.

There should be a clear and consistent credit policy. Senior management should provide guidelines to credit controllers about:

- refusing credit to certain categories of customer
- credit limits for customers in a particular rating category
- total credit limits.

Policy decisions should be reviewed continually, and the credit granted by a company or a bank must be affordable. Credit policy should not be allowed to undermine the financial position of the company.

There must be a system for assessing the creditworthiness of individual customers in order to make decisions about granting credit. Individual customers should be monitored continually, and their credit limits reassessed. The external and inhouse sources of information for carrying out this task have been described in earlier chapters.

The order processing and debt collection operations must be efficient. These operational activities are considered in *Framework for Credit Risk Management*, another title in the series, and include, for example, query control and chasing late payments.

It is also important to monitor and control the system itself. Credit managers should be given targets or budgets, against which their performance should be measured. Performance reports can include information about late payments, e.g. average debtor days or days' sales outstanding, bad debts written off, credit utilization, and so on.

Measuring credit risk should be a process of monitoring individual customers, and comparing actual performance against target measures within policy guidelines.

Measuring Risk

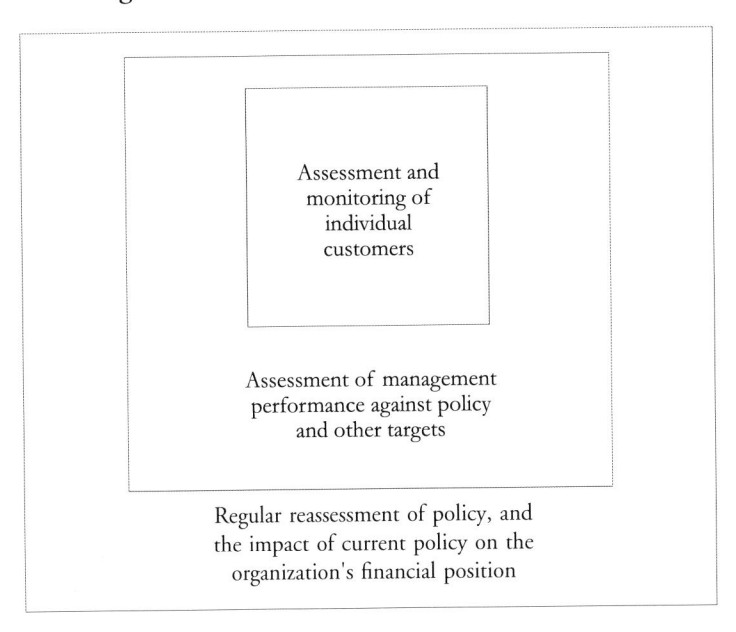

| Assessment and monitoring of individual customers |
| Assessment of management performance against policy and other targets |
| Regular reassessment of policy, and the impact of current policy on the organization's financial position |

Measurement and Judgment

The creditworthiness of a customer can be measured, in the sense that financial ratios can be calculated from the customer's accounts. Credit ratings can be given to categorize the credit standing of a company. A points-scoring system can be used to measure a customer's payment record or to set customer credit limits. A bank can measure its risk assets, and the risk asset ratio of a bank can be monitored.

Despite these methods of measuring risk, credit assessment is largely qualitative, and a matter of judgment. In practice, many bankers and corporate credit managers use credit information to reach an informed judgment rather than a measured conclusion.

Credit ratings, for example, are often used to support a lending decision or a decision to grant credit, but not to impose strict guidelines. Bankers and corporate credit managers will base their decision on a judgment about the customer's competence and integrity, and simply look for justification and support from credit measures such as ratings or ratio analysis. If a debt is unpaid, the credit manager can justify his original credit decision, using the defense that he shouldn't be blamed for someone else's opinion of the customer's credit rating.

Example 1
Omega Bank decides to lend $20 million to Alpha, a single-A rated company, at an interest rate of 1% above LIBOR. If Alpha subsequently goes into liquidation, the banker who made the lending decision can justify his action on the grounds that Alpha had a good credit rating.

Example 2
The credit controller of Beta agrees to grant credit of $25,000 to a customer, Gamma. Information from a credit reference agency indicates that Gamma has a reasonable payment record, paying its debts on average within 30 days of the due date.

Gamma subsequently fails to pay an invoice for $20,000.

The credit controller, to justify his decision to allow credit to Gamma, can point to the credit rating supplied by the agency.

Judgment can be such an overriding factor that lending decisions can be taken in spite of the credit information available. Banks, for example, have been accused at times, justifiably or not, of a shared-misery-for-all approach to lending. In other words, if other banks are lending to a dubious or risky customer, the risk must be lower than it seems, and if the debt has to be written off, at least all the other banks would be in the same position.

Banks and corporate credit managers also can be inclined to the view that a customer is too big or too important to fail, and although payment could be late, the customer eventually will pay. Credit is therefore granted whenever the customer asks for it, and late payments are tolerated. With large customers, a small supplier could decide that there is no choice but to give the customer whatever credit is demanded, in the expectation or hope that the debt eventually will be paid.

Finding the Right Balance

A balance has to be struck between judgment and objective measurement in credit decisions. Although decisions rely on judgment at an operational or management level, the value of credit measurement and monitoring systems should be recognized. Judgment should be based on informed, measured opinion, using suitable sources for credit analysis and measurement. Management should then be held responsible, within a reporting system, for the judgments they have made.

Glossary

Aged Debtors' Report
Report listing overdue debts and the length of time for which they have been overdue.

Basle Agreement
International agreement by central banks, members of the Bank for International Settlements, about minimum capital adequacy requirements for banks. Also called the BIS rules.

Capital Adequacy
Having enough long-term capital to be financially secure. With reference to a bank, capital adequacy means having enough capital funds to protect it from the risk that customers could lose their deposits as a result of trading losses, e.g. from bad debts by the bank.

Cash flow Projection
Estimate of the future cash flows or a future cash position of a business, often prepared by applying assumptions for the future to historical revenues and costs.

Chapter 11
Chapter 11 of the US Bankruptcy Code, that permits an insolvent company to file for protection from its creditors. The company can then continue in business, working to a reorganization plan approved by the court.

Country Risk
The risk that the financial position of organizations in a particular country and their ability to pay debts could be affected by changes or developments in that country.

Creative Accounting
The use of favorable accounting policies to prepare a profit and loss account and balance sheet. Creative accounting methods can be used to improve reported profits and asset values, and can disguise a company's true financial position.

Credit Bureau
Organization that provides credit information about businesses to clients.

Credit Rating
A measured judgment, or formal opinion, about the likelihood that interest payments on a particular issue of bonds or other debt security will be paid in full and on time, and that the debt principal will be repaid in full at maturity. Ratings are provided by specialist agencies. The highest credit rating for long-term debt is AAA (triple-A).

Credit Reference Agency
See Credit Bureau.

Credit Scoring
Assessing the creditworthiness of a business by giving it a score based on key attributes or financial ratios.

Credit Watch
Monitoring by a rating agency of the credit rating for an organization's debt, with a view to altering the rating. Also called rating watch.

Currency Bloc
Group of countries with domestic currencies whose exchange rates are closely tied to a major currency, e.g. there is a dollar bloc of countries and a deutschemark bloc.

Dividend Cover
The ratio of income after tax to dividends. For example, a dividend is covered twice when income after tax is twice as large as the dividends to stockholders.

Exposure
A financial risk facing a business that can be categorized according to its cause or source, e.g. credit risk exposures.

Financial Flexibility
Ability to raise money from alternative sources, e.g. sale of fixed assets, new loans, should the main source of cash inflows, normally trading income, be insufficient.

Financial Risk
The risk of profits being affected by unexpected changes in financial conditions or circumstances. The term can be applied to a company's borrowings and financial leverage, and is the risk that the company's

profits could be insufficient to meet interest payments and other obligations.

Industry Risk
Risk arising from the likelihood that all businesses in a particular industry could be affected by an economic downturn in the industry.

Insolvency
Inability to pay debts. Procedures in the event of insolvency vary from country to country. A company goes into liquidation (Chapter 7 bankruptcy) or files for protection under Chapter 11 of the Bankruptcy Code.

Liquidation
Process of winding up a company and bringing its affairs to an end. A liquidator is appointed to carry out this task.

Liquidity Run
A sudden increase in cash expenditures, creating potential cash flow (liquidity) difficulties for the company affected.

Marginal Customer
An extra customer. Companies seeking growth will try to sell to new customers, often customers of a different type. These marginal customers could be a higher credit risk than the company's existing customer base.

Marginal Lending
Further Lending. This can be extra lending to existing customers or loans to new customers.

Minimum Leverage Ratio
A capital adequacy requirement, calling for the value of a bank's capital funds to be not less than a certain proportion of its assets.

Minimum-Risk Assets Ratio
Capital adequacy requirement, whereby a bank's capital funds must be not less in value than a certain proportion of its risk assets.
See also Risk Assets.

Overtrading
Over-reliance on short-term credit to finance business operations. Overtrading can be evident in rapidly growing businesses that delay payments to creditors and use a bank overdraft facility to its limit.

Priority Expenditures
Payments that must be made to avoid the immediate risk of liquidation. In addition to payments for normal trading expenditures, e.g. payments of wages and salaries, they include payments of interest and taxation.

Rating Watch
See Credit Watch.

Receivership
This is a UK term and is the process by which unpaid secured creditors of a company appoint a receiver. A receiver takes on responsibility for the management and disposal of the assets over which the creditors have a charge. Proceeds from the disposal of the assets are paid to the secured creditors by the receiver. Receivership often leads to the liquidation of the company.

Reserve Accounting
Accounting practice of recording gains or losses or expenditures as increases or reductions in a reserve account, rather than as items of profit or loss or expense in the annual profit and loss account.

Risk Assets
Assets of a bank, adjusted by a weighting from 0% to 100% to allow for their risk, i.e. the possibility that the bank could suffer losses from the assets.

Status Report
Detailed report about the financial position and payment record of a company. Status reports can be provided by a credit reference bureau or a bank.

Tier 1 Capital
Core capital of a bank, consisting of share capital and reserves, excluding revaluation reserves.

Tier 2 Capital
Capital of a bank that is not core capital.

Trade Reference
Reference given by another supplier on behalf of a potential new customer. The reference should indicate the period of time during which the supplier has had a trading relationship with the customer and the reliability of the customer in paying debts over that time.

Triple-A
Highest credit rating given to long-term debt by the major credit rating agencies Standard & Poor's, Moody's and Fitch IBCA.

Working Capital
A term commonly used to mean stocks, debtors and creditors. By this definition, stocks plus debtors minus creditors equals working capital.

Z Score
A measured assessment of a company's financial situation, and the possibility that it might fail. Z scores are derived from a corporate failure prediction model, using key financial ratios.

Index

Adverse trading 7, 8
Aged debtors' exception report 99
Aged debtors' report 99
Amortization 57
Annual expenditure 8
Asian crisis 28, 39
Assessing country risk 67
Assessment of banks 74-90

Bad debt risk 13
Bad loans 10
Balance sheet structure 29
Balance sheet values 17
Bank failures 75
Bank status reports 47
Banker's reference 17
Bankruptcies 25
Bankruptcy code 109
Bankruptcy petition 34
Basle agreement 18, 79-82, 83-84
Behavorial scoring 54
BIS agreement 79
Borrowing money 88
Building company profiles 51-54
Bureaux 46
Business failure 13
Business risk 17, 27

Capital adequacy 18, 76-79
Capital commitments 9
Capital expenditure 55
Capital funding 7
Capital strength 50
Capitalizing development costs 10

Capitalizing interest costs 10
Cash flow adjustments 57
Cash flow crisis 8
Cash flow projections 51, 54-61
Cash rich companies 16
Chapter 11 109-113
Chapter 11 rules 110
Collateral security 76
Commitment fees 74
Company loans 5
Confirmed letters of credit 20
Contingent liabilities 30
Contractual payments 29
Control limits 69
Controlling credit risk 2-14
Corporate credit controller 46
Corporate credit risk analysis 50-51
Corporate customer 19
Cost of sales 55, 56
Country limit 20
Country risk 27, 64-72
Court judgments 45
Creative accounting 7, 10
Credit analysis 7
Credit analysis on banks 85-86
Credit analysts 18
Credit assessment 16-22
Credit assessments 13
Credit bureau reports 45
Credit bureaux 43-47
Credit decisions 16, 20
Credit deterioration 21, 106-114
Credit exposure 3, 4
Credit information 42

INDEX

Credit information agency 19
Credit insurance 71
Credit limits for currency blocs 71
Credit limits for individual countries 95
Credit management 6
Credit managers 5, 7, 13
Credit protection 71
Credit quality 37, 38
Credit rating agencies 24-40
Credit rating agencies 39-40
Credit rating process 26
Credit rating system 16, 24
Credit reference agencies 16, 42, 46
Credit risk 77
Credit risk assessment 13
Credit scoring 53
Credit watch 38
Credit worthiness 24
Credit granting process 7
Credit risk insurance 20
Credit scoring model 20
Credit scoring system 53
Currency risk 65, 66
Cut-off scores 53
Cycle of credit monitoring 106
Cyclical business 28

Debt capital 24
Debt issuer 40
Debt protection levels 27
Debt securities 25, 32
Debtor's assets 4
Default 37, 38
Deposit limits 16
Depositing money 87
Depreciation policies 29
Direct loss 4
Distribution costs 55, 56
Dividend cover 51
Dividend payout ratio 55
Duration of credit risk 3-4

Eastern bloc countries 39
Economic conditions 6
Economic cycles 28, 64

Economic depression 66
Economic growth 69
Economic risk 65
Environmental factors 64
Equity capital 29
Equity finance 31
Eurobonds 24
Excessive capital commitments 9
Exchange controls 66
Existing debt 16
External agency 19
External assessment methods 18
External assessments 17, 40
External information sources 42-48

Faulty credit analysis 10
Financial assessment 17-20
Financial collapse 69
Financial flexibility 29
Financial rating analysis 28
Financial ratio analysis 17, 18, 50, 108
Financial ratios 26
Fitch IBCA ratings 35-38
Fixed assets 10, 20
Fixed charge cover 29
Fixed costs 8
Floating assets 20
Forced sale risk 77
Foreign exchange markets 71
Formal credit rating 26
Forward rate agreements 2
FRAs 2
Fund managers 24
FX transaction 25

Government agencies 16, 24
Government interference 28
Gross income 56

High credit quality 37, 38
High default risk 37, 38
Highly speculative 37
High risk regions 70
Historical accounting 17, 44

Implied debt rating 28
Income bonds 34
Indicators of credit deterioration 107-109
Indirect loss 4
Individual credit transactions 21
Individual rating 35
Industrial reports 65
Industrial unrest 66
Industry limit 20
Industry risk 27, 64-72
Industry risk analysis 28
In house assessment 19
In house credit analysis 17
In house credit assessments 49-62
In house credit ratings 96
Insolvencies 45
Inter-company comparisons 29
Inter-company loans 12
Interest cover 31
Interest payments 2
Interest rates 55
Internal assessment methods 18
International credit ratings 36
International settlements 79
Investment analysts 18
Investment policy 24
Investment risk 77
Issue of bonds 25
Issued debt capital 31

Junk bond status 70, 75

Key cash flow ratios 29
Labor unrest 28
Large-scale borrower 19
Legal guarantee 35
Letters of credit 2
LIBOR 24
Liquid assets 85
Liquidation 74
Liquidity 85
Liquidity run 7, 9
Loan covenants 11
Loan guarantees 20

Loan principal 58
Loan principal repayments 2
Long-term risk 68

Marginal lending 5
Marginal trade credit 5
Market surveys 65
Measurement and judgment 118-119
Measuring risk 117
Minimum risk asset ratio 76, 77, 80
Minimum leverage ratio 76, 77, 80
Monitoring credit 98-102
Moody's debt rating 30-32

National debt 68
Negative cash flow 58
Net cash flow 8
Non-core business 29

Operating leases 29
Operating profit 29
Operational cash flow 58
Over-trading 7

Payment score 46
Performance bonds 2
Points-scoring system 17
Political risk 65
Potential bad debt 42
Potential credit risk 5
Potential value 13
Preference dividends 29
Preliminary assessment 26
Product market analysis 28
Profit and loss account 10
Providers of credit 16
Provision accounting 30
Public information 44
Public relations 25
Purpose of credit ratings 24-25

Rating exercise 25
Rating process for a company 26-30
Recession 64
Regulatory risk 65

INDEX

Reserve accounting 10, 30
Risk analysis reports 67
Risk and banks 68
Risk and companies 69
Risk and return 5-6
Risk-weighted assets 79

Sales 55
Setting and policing credit
 limits 92-104
Settlement discount 46
Share price 51
Size of credit risk 3-4
Sources of assessments 16-17
Sources of credit information 19
Sovereign rating 32
Specialist agencies 16, 25
Specific debt issue 25
Speculative 37
Speculative grades 34, 37
Split rating 34
Standard & Poor's 32-34
Standing starting credit limits 96
Statistical techniques 53
Status reports 45
Support rating 35
Surplus assets 29
Swaps 2

Tax payments 55
Tier 1 capital 80
Tier 2 capital 80
Total credit limit 93
Total credit limits 100
Trade debt 4
Trade debtors 5
Trade references 47
Trading outlook 51

Uncovered dividend 52
Unsecured creditors 4
Using bank risk information 86
Using financial assessments 20-21

Variable costs 8
Volatile revenue dynamic 64
Volume of sales 6

Warning signs of credit risk 6-13
Working capital changes 57
Working capital management 55
Write-downs 89

Z score assessments 20
Z scoring 20

131